Teacher's Handbook
of Special Learning Problems
and How to Handle Them

Also by the Author

Successful Methods for Teaching the Slow Learner, Muriel Karlin
and Regina Berger
The Effective Student Activities Program, Muriel Karlin and
Regina Berger
*Discipline and the Disruptive Child: A Practical Guide for Elemen-
tary Teachers*, Muriel Karlin and Regina Berger
*Experiential Learning: An Effective Teaching Program for Elemen-
tary Schools*, Muriel Karlin and Regina Berger
*Individualizing Instruction: Complete Guide for Planning, Teaching
and Evaluation*, Muriel Karlin and Regina Berger
Administrator's Guide to a Practical Career Education Program
Classroom Activities Desk Book for Fun and Learning
*Administering and Teaching Sex Education in the Elementary
School*

Teacher's Handbook
of Special Learning Problems
and How to Handle Them

Muriel Schoenbrun Karlin

Parker Publishing Company, Inc.

West Nyack, New York

Library of Congress Cataloging in Publication Data

Karlin, Muriel Schoenbrun.
    Teacher's handbook of special learning problems and
how to handle them.

    Includes index.
    1. Elementary school teaching. I. Title.
LB1715.K25   372.1'1'02   77-23217
ISBN 0-13-888420-X

Printed in the United States of America

DEDICATION

To Len, who has worked long and hard on this manuscript after putting in long and hard days working at his own profession, and without whom I could never be me, this book is lovingly dedicated.

How This Book Will Help

You Solve Learning Problems

All of us are aware of the many problems teachers must cope with in the course of a day's work. The problems vary—from the child who is having reading difficulties to the class in chaos, with all of the gradations in between. This book will help you *solve* these problems, and it is likely that you will keep it on your desk and turn to it constantly. You can be certain that no matter what problems you have you are not alone.

This book is a compilation of tested solutions to these problems, based on the author's nearly twenty years of personal experience as classroom teacher, guidance counselor, and supervisor. The author is still actively engaged in supervision in an intermediate school with 1,500 children. This school is a microcosm of the "melting pot" community in which it is located, with pupils from every socio-economic and ethnic background. The solutions in this book are directly related to problems we face (and the same problems you are faced with) every day of the school year.

All of the suggestions in this book are directly related to the solution of a problem. When you have a problem, you need to know what action to take, and you'll find it in these pages.

When letters and notes will help, you will find appropriate pages in this book which may be duplicated for your use. When learning materials for use in an opaque projector can be used effectively, they are included. The plastic comb binding makes this book easy to place on the machine and easy to project.

We begin with learning problems that relate to the "average" child, the slow learner, and the bright child. Much has been written and said about the slow learner, but the other types of children are equally deserving of your time and attention. They may not require the amount of time and attention your slow learners do, but they should be taken into consideration and their instruction planned for. We then go into detail in three subject areas: reading, arithmetic, and language arts. We depend to a large extent on diagnosis—on finding the level of a child's achievement and building on that. By learning what a child's needs are, you are better able to meet them. You can learn, for example, by a survey of the compositions your children write, what their needs are—in terms of written English. You can then teach them sentence structure by abstracting their errors from the written work and correcting them. You will learn techniques for teaching vocabulary in each and every subject area, because without word knowledge your children cannot communicate ideas.

The next section will help you establish a climate for learning in your classroom. When you manage your class efficiently, you can utilize pupils' work to a great extent and leave more time for actual teaching. This concept is covered in detail, including methods for having your pupils mark their test papers. (They don't mark their own, they mark their classmates'.) We believe that giving pupils responsibilities, besides being a big help to you, does a great deal for them in terms of helping them develop and mature. Many teachers want to know how to plan but are in a quandary when asked to show their lesson plans. Because of this, we also cover planning on a long-term basis, planning on a unit basis, and planning a daily basis. Individualization and grouping are also included, with specific guidelines to help you in planning ways to meet children's needs.

If your school is suffering from budget cuts, or if you would like to obtain more materials than you already have, you will find many sources of free materials. This book will be helpful in teaching you to make your own materials, to have your students make them, and to use materials which are usually readily available, such as magazines and newspapers.

The third section of this book deals with pupil behavior. It contains many methods that will help you establish a viable teaching situation in your classroom. Realizing that there are many different types of problems, we categorize them and give you solutions which have been successful—ranging from teaching the "Golden Rule" to methods for breaking up a fight. We show ways to cope with specific types of problems, such as hyperactive children, disruptive children, and youngsters who are psychologically ill. We consider the child whose self-image is poor and whose behavior and achievement suffer as a result.

This book concentrates on real problems and practical solutions. Our children are our most valuable national resource—and they are placed in our hands. This book will help you to make the most of every one of your teaching minutes.

Muriel Schoenbrun Karlin

ACKNOWLEDGMENTS

It is impossible to thank everyone who has had a hand—or an idea—in this book. However, I would be remiss if I did not mention certain individuals, and I would like to thank the following people:

Mr. Norman H. Harris, Principal, Anning S. Prall Intermediate School, Staten Island, New York; Mr. Joseph N. Marone, Assistant Principal, and the members of the Language Arts department of that school.

Mr. Irving Dickson, for his work and for the posters of the "Golden Deeds."

Mr. Emanuel Trachman, for the photographs which appear in this book.

Ms. Meredith DeGood of the Columbia School, Peoria, Illinois, for her unit in career education.

Mrs. Helen Harris, who was for many years my personal guidance counselor.

Ms. Regina Berger, for the educational background and interest she has always given me.

Mr. Joseph Kass, a student at Susan Wagner High School, Staten Island, for his help in the preparation of the manuscript.

Mrs. Branda Smith, for her editorial work and secretarial skills.

Dr. Leonard Karlin, my husband, for his work on the manuscript and for his discussions of it with me.

The students and faculty of Anning S. Prall Intermediate School with whom I am privileged to work. I hope I have been a source of inspiration to them as they certainly have been to me.

M.S.K.

Table of Contents

How to Get the Max __um Achievement from Your
Intellectually Gifted Students *(cont'd.)*

Chapter 1

How to Get the Average Child

to Learn and to Achieve

One of the major characteristics of teaching is that it requires constant problem solving. We're faced with decision making almost on a minute-to-minute basis. Probably the greatest problem we're confronted with is: "How can we get *them* to work and to learn?" For most teachers, "them" refers to the average child, and it is for that reason we've begun this book with that problem—How can you get the average child to learn and to achieve? How can you get the majority of your class to participate actively in the learning process?

Let's begin by defining our terms. What is an "average" child? We'll call "average" those children who are reading from about one year below grade level to one year above. They are the ones who score from 90 to 110 on intelligence tests. But let's look at nonacademic criteria. The average child is more interested in watching television than reading and, indeed, watches TV approximately three hours per day. In the teen years he is more involved in sports that in any other activity, and she's more interested in boys. School is rarely among their favorite pastimes, although most of them accept it good-naturedly. However, it is our task to teach them—and that's what this chapter is all about.

How to Motivate Average Children

Our children are very different from those of previous generations. Many things have influenced them, television being one of the foremost. For legions of youngsters, the television has been their first teacher, and, in some respects, a fairly good one at that. These children are growing up in a period of great social unrest, and this, too, must certainly be taken into consideration. We cannot expect them to sit and listen to us. They won't! We cannot expect them to walk into our classrooms and respect us simply because we are teachers. They won't. But we can—and we must—motivate them to learn. Motivate—the magic word—the key to all learning.

Let's look into a classroom:

"Today," a teacher is saying, "we're going to begin our unit on Egypt." He darkens the room, lights several candles, and instructs the children to close their eyes until he tells them to open them. Out from a closet, where it had been carefully hidden, he takes a mummy! Oh, not a real mummy, but one realistic enough to have the children gasp audibly! The teacher proceeds to talk about the mummy and then about Tutankhamen and the curse. He spends almost an entire period on this introduction. What would you expect the reaction to be? Of course the kids are entranced. But more than that, they're motivated to learn about all the mysteries (and all the facts—because they're related to the mysteries) of ancient Egypt. (Where did the "mummy" come from? Several of the children had made it the previous year. "We have a group produce a mummy each year," the teacher points out. "They love doing it, and I love using it.")

Far out? Theatrical? You bet! Motivation? Superb.

To motivate your average children, to involve them, set up mysteries. Pose every topic as a question for which they are seeking an answer.

One science teacher took her entire class out to the street where her car was parked. She opened the hood, and every child looked at the engine. For many it was a brand-new experience. She got into her car, pressed the gas pedal, and nothing happened. She did this several times. Still nothing. And she said nothing. This was repeated four or five times, until one child shrieked, "You didn't turn the key! You didn't turn the key!" That was the beginning of a unit on the automobile engine.

Motivation can be achieved through dramatics, mysteries, challenges, games, and gimmicks. But if you place material on the board and say, "Copy this and learn it for the test on Tuesday," your students won't learn it.

We will be discussing learning in terms of two basic types of learning—skills and knowledge. Skills are a series of specific actions a person has learned. They may be reading or math skills, typing skills, or car repairing skills. Knowledge is the possession of facts of a simple or complex nature. Both skills and knowledge are used in problem solving. However, in teaching them our methods will differ. If you motivate by offering problems for your children to solve, you stimulate the use of both skills and knowledge—and you can make the youngsters anxious to use them.

Case History of an "Average" Child

Clementine has an IQ of 99. She has gotten C's or B's throughout her school career. She's neat, clean, and outgoing when she's with her friends. Her reading score was on grade level until the fifth grade, when she scored 6.5. That year her grades went up in every subject. The next year she returned to her previous pattern of C's and a few B's.

In interviewing her parents, we learned of no significant events at home to account for her sudden improvement. But then her mother clarified the situation: "Clem loved that teacher. She could really get her to work. She had that effect on all the children."

The effect we, as teachers, have on our students is sometimes amazing. It can range from a totally negative one to an extremely positive one. One highly successful elementary school teacher told us that she feels her successful results are due to her conference system. "I manage to have a conference with every child at least once a month. That's not even difficult, because it averages out to one or two per day. I use the time when the children are reading their library books—what we call 'free reading.' "

The conferences she holds are very important, because, among other things, she builds the youngsters' self-confidence. "I can always find some aspect of their work to praise," she says. "Then I ask, 'Have you anything you'd like to talk about?' Girls are better able to open up than boys, but I've found that I can get the boys to do so, too."

The children understand that not only is this young woman their teacher, but she is also a friend who is interested in them. The conference continues with a discussion of the child's work, special projects, or suggestions.

Average youngsters need their teacher's personal attention. The disruptive ones get it almost automatically. The bright children sometimes demand it, but the average ones rarely do. Yet the average children need this attention just as much.

On the intermediate school level, individual attention is more difficult—but it's not impossible. Taking the time to get to know students can often make a huge difference in their achievement level.

Many teachers use an autobiographical approach. They ask their students to write a completely confidential autobiography which includes questions such as:

1. Where (what geographical area) were you born? When?
2. How many people do you live with? How are they related to you and how do you get along with them?
3. If you could go anywhere or do anything you'd like to do, where would you go and what would you do?
4. If you could become anything in the world you want when you grow up, what would you choose?
5. When do you feel happiest?
6. When do you feel saddest?
7. What do you like most about yourself?
8. What do you like least? (What would you change if you could?)
9. What is your biggest problem?
10. What do you think is the greatest problem the people of the world face today?

Assure your children that their replies are entirely

confidential—but that they are a way to introduce themselves to you. (Incidentally, try filling out this questionnaire yourself. You may be surprised at some of your own replies.)

Discuss the responses with the children privately. Each will assume an identity and a status in your mind. Try this and see if it doesn't happen. Your "average" child won't be "just average" anymore.

How to Raise Aspirations

One day we invited a gentleman to speak to some of our eighth grade students. His topic was "Going into Business for Yourself." His name is Walter Geier, and the organization he represents is the Institute for Free Enterprise. His entire presentation was so electrifying and dynamic that every child was impressed. But, more important, he introduced a concept that few of the children had known anything about. Several of their parents were in business, but even those youngsters knew little about being entrepreneurs.

To raise career aspirations, bring career education into your classroom. There are some children who aspire to professions— usually because their parents are already professionals. Most youngsters, however, have little knowledge about the world of work or what it takes to succeed in it.

As an interesting experiment, give your children the quiz in Figure 1-1.

Most teachers are very surprised by the results they get on this quiz. It becomes obvious that in order to raise aspirations, we must introduce goals which our children can work toward. If a child has never been introduced to engineering, how can he or she ever aim for it?

The average child needs this type of information. Teaching it as a problem for them to solve is easy. After the children have indicated a career preference, tell them: "Your problem now is to learn about the career you listed in answer to Question #1. Talk to people, read books, check through filmstrips and films. Find out what a person in that career does—how he spends his days. Learn as much as you can about that career!"

Think about these questions carefully before you answer.

1. What do you expect to do to earn a living when you are old enough to do so?
2. Why did you select that job? What do you like about it?
3. What education or training will you need?
4. Where can you get that training?
5. After a person finishes high school, how long (how many years) does he have to study to become:
   a. a veterinarian
   b. a truck driver
   c. a doctor
   d. a teacher
   e. a factory inspector
6. What does each of the following persons do?
   a. an accountant
   b. a social worker
   c. a laboratory technician
   d. a mason
   e. a beautician
7. How can a person become:
   a. a professional ball player
   b. a stewardess
   c. a clown
   d. a brick layer
   e. a nurse
8. How can a person prepare to be president of the United States?

Figure 1-1

How to Get Average Students Involved in What Is Going on in the Classroom

We frequently receive complaints from students ranging from "Johnny is bothering me" to "I hate the teacher." But very rarely is the complaint that the teacher is overworking the class. More often it's because, "That teacher doesn't give us enough work. He's wasting time." Our own daughter complained bitterly of a teacher who took the time to talk about her husband's personal habits (including the size of underwear he wore).

If you have work going on all the time and it is not too difficult, most of your students will do it. For the few who don't, you may have to insist—but most of them will work if challenged.

Challenge the children. Thinking up challenges is, in itself, a challenge for you—but it is one which is eminently worthwhile, because it encourages your class to think and work.

We saw one teacher hold up a stamp and then pass it around so that each child could study it. He then asked the class to figure out the story behind it. The stamp was "The Four Chaplains" (issued May 28, 1948, Scott #956), and it introduced a unit on World War II. There is scarcely a great American or a great event that is not commemorated on a stamp.

Challenge the children with games and puzzles. For example, to teach the concept "A noun is the name of a person, place, or thing," hold a contest. The winner is the pupil who can list the most nouns beginning with the same letter. He or she can choose the letter, but all the words must begin with it. (Usually, most of the class selects "A.") Allow the use of dictionaries at times. At other times play the same game without the use of any reference book.

All of the parts of speech can be taught this way, as well as prefixes, roots, and suffixes.

Use behavior modification. When you want to drill math factors, for example, reward correct results. If a student does 15 simple problems correctly, he receives a clue toward discovering "hidden treasure." The more correct results a student arrives at, the more clues he will get. Ultimately, each child is able to locate his own prize. It takes the teacher time to conceal the clues and treasures, but the children enjoy it—and work!

Challenge student creativity. One teacher in a sixth grade language arts class had each of her pupils write a short statement on subjects such as "Happiness is . . . ," "Fun is . . . ," and "People are . . . ." The children really got into the spirit. The challenge was to put a lot of meaning into very few words.

How to Present New Material

Your interest and enthusiasm can make any subject you choose come to life. However, every subject must be treated with sensitivity.

One teacher was teaching the "melting pot" concept. He divided the class into groups and had each group make a party. The Chinese members of the class did a celebration of Chinese New Year, complete with dragon. The Jewish children made a "bar mitzvah," and the Irish children made a corned beef and cabbage dinner. The enthusiasm of the class, and of the teacher, was tremendous.

Present your new material with dramatic flair. If you're enjoying your teaching, it's almost guaranteed that your children will too.

Present lots of material. Your children may not learn all of it, but they will get some, and often they will learn more than you expect. After you've made your presentation, put what you expect them to learn on the board for them to copy. Your class secretary can do this for you quite effectively. Don't overload the board with hundreds of words. Many teachers use an outline form for this purpose very successfully.

This written material serves several purposes. It causes you to select and emphasize the main points you have covered. It acts as a summary. It gives your children material to study—for reinforcement and reiteration.

We have been told by students, "Mrs. R. is so good! She gives us stuff to study, and when she gives us a test, that's what's on the test."

How to Make Students Responsible for Their Work

It's our opinion that a lack of development of feelings of responsibility has had the greatest detrimental effect on our educational system.

How can we develop this sense of responsibility?

1.   Let the children know exactly what they are responsible for in terms of work, behavior, and personal characteristics. "You're responsible for knowing the water cycle," you say to your science class. "If you don't understand it, please raise your hand now or see me later."

Once they know what they are responsible for, it's your responsibility to see that they can carry it through. Therefore, you vary the work. You may assign five spelling words to some youngsters, ten to others, and fifteen or even twenty to others.

By using this system of varied responsibilities, you can meet the needs of all children. However, don't make the work too easy. Most children need to be pushed, to be instilled with the desire and the need *to have to do more.*

2.   Treat your youngsters as mature (for their age level, of course) human beings. Even fourth graders can be taught the words "mature," "immature," and "responsibility" and will be able to handle them and what they entail. Perhaps there will be some who really aren't mature enough, but we have seen very surprising results from this approach. Education must be concerned with the development of attitudes. In your classroom, you can develop these attitudes and make teaching far easier. All children want to be "mature"—you only have to help them to see themselves in that light.

3.   Once you have established responsibility, it's up to you to check to see that the work is done or the proper behavior displayed. Expect to lose in some cases but to win in many.

Unfortunately, not all adults live up to their responsibilities. You only have to look at statistics to see this borne out. How many adults don't bother to vote? How many men fail to pay child support? We mention this so that you do not expect too much of your children and so that you'll realize the need for constant checking.

Checking may be done in a variety of ways. One teacher has youngsters walk down the aisles, checking their classmates' work.

"I choose a different youngster each day—one from each row. One day it will be the child sitting in the third seat of each row. Another day, it will be the child in the first seat, and so on. Works beautifully. Of course, some days I do the checking myself."

Another teacher collects assignments religiously. "I found," he said, "that at the beginning of the year only 75% of the class responded. The first week it was 100%, but it dropped to 75% rapidly. But by collecting, grading (I use Outstanding, Satisfactory, or Unsatisfactory—I simply read the papers and stamp them with a rubber stamp which says O, S, or U), and returning the papers, I've changed that 75% to 95%. There are still some children who 'forget' or who don't bother. The number does decrease. I also talk a lot about responsibility."

For those teachers who use individualized methods, such as contracts or committee work, inculcating responsibility is, of course, every bit as important.

4.   Grades and other rewards are definitely part of the development of responsibility.

"They didn't do the required work, so I gave them 60's," one teacher reported. (This is in an intermediate school.) "I assigned a paper. It was a long assignment, and it determined their entire grade for the month. Many of these kids are on the Honor Roll, or would have been, but this failure prevented it. They can't believe it. But I told them that it was their responsibility to write a paper and mine to fail them if they didn't." Fortunately, we've known very few teachers who feel this way.

5.   Many teachers ask students to grade themselves. It's an interesting experiment and one that we recommend to you. The grade a child gives himself or herself reflects his or her self-image to a great extent. If the child thinks well of himself or herself, it's reflected here. Generally the grades are quite appropriate.

How to Reinforce Learning

You will find that if you develop feelings of responsibility, reinforcement of learning is partially taken care of. However, some children need help in both understanding and retention.

We have found that it is sometimes necessary to teach the same subject in a variety of ways. Some children will respond immediately. Others will require different explanations. Still others will need repetition. But it is often necessary to cover the same concept again and again.

By giving your children notes to study from and telling them how to study, you can help them develop good habits which remain with them until the ends of their lives.

We wrote the following article for our newspaper column in the *Staten Island Advance*. It was written for older students, but the same basic methods can be used by your pupils. One of the complaints we hear from many people is, "I don't know how to study." It's true. This column has been duplicated and distributed many times. One parent reported that she taped it to her son's mirror.

Tailor Ways of Study
So That They Work Best for You.

1. If you do your studying only to please your teacher or to do well on tests, you cheat yourself. You will get out of this only what you put into it. The first rule is: put your mind on what you are studying. If you give it your attention, you will find that the material will stick; but if you daydream or become diverted, your time will not be as productive.

2. Try to interest yourself in your assignments. Find things in them which are of interest to you.

3. Set aside a definite time and place to study. Don't leave your work until late in the evening. When you are tired it is much more difficult to study than it is when you are fresh. Many college students stay up half the night, usually just before an examination, studying. It is far better to go to bed at a reasonable hour and to get up at five in the morning. (If you try this system, make sure that you "wake up" before starting to work.)

(For younger children, the early hours of the evening are preferable—not just after they have come home from school. They're tired from the day's routine when they get home, and they need a break. If the weather is good, playing outdoors is an excellent activity. If the weather is poor, relaxation is still necessary for several hours. Then, when they start their homework or studying, they are refreshed.)

4. If you can find a quiet place, use it. If not, it may be necessary for you to use the public library or an area in your school reserved for study.

There are many young people who maintain that they can study well with their study areas filled with music. This is an individual matter. If you find you can, fine. If your grades indicate that you aren't doing so well, try working in a quiet place and see if that doesn't help you.

5. Have everything you need available. This includes textbooks, notebooks, papers, pens, and pencils. Try not to jump up and down constantly to get things you have forgotten.

6. Start to work immediately. It has been said by one famous failure, "Work fascinates me. I could look at it for hours." Don't just look at your work. Begin as soon as you sit down.

7. Determine exactly what you must do to complete your assignment. If you are told to study it, to learn it, or that you are having a test on it, use the following methods:

. . . Read all of the material for which you are responsible. This material may be in your notebook or in a textbook.

. . . Think about the material. (What is it all about? Why is it important? What are the most important ideas?)

. . . Be sure that you understand the material before trying to really learn it. If you don't, try to figure it out. If you can't, you have several alternatives: Look it up—in your textbook or in an encyclopedia. Ask your parents or other family members. Call another person in your class and ask him. Wait until you see your teacher and ask him or her.

. . . Now, assuming that you understand everything you have to learn, take the material and divide it into small segments of from four to six items. We call these "groupettes."

. . . Give each "groupette" a title. What is the main thought? That is usually the best title. But you may want to call the groupette something else that means more to you. The name you give it is not important, but giving it one is.

. . . For each groupette, figure out:

What holds this groupette together? In what ways are the items related? (As you progress in school, your groupettes will come to contain more items, but otherwise the technique remains the same.)

How can you learn the groupette? There are three methods: reading, writing, or reading aloud.

Learning the groupettes by reading:

Read one groupette at a time. Think about it. Read every item until you feel you know it.

On a sheet of paper, write the name of the groupette and the items in it. Check these against your original. If you have them all correct, go on to the next groupette.

Learning the groupettes by writing:

Instead of reading one group at a time, make a list of the names of all of the groupettes. Then read the entire batch of material and put the paper away. See how many items you can write under each groupette name. Write in as many as you can. When you have written in as many as possible, check your work against the original list. Fill in each groupette. Put all of these papers away and start the process over again. Do this until you can fill in every item in every groupette. You will then have learned all of the material.

This method takes lots of scrap paper and patience. But it is better than the reading method for many people, because you cannot fool yourself into thinking that you have learned everything. You must write it fully, and there can be no question about the results.

Learning the groupettes by reading aloud:

This method consists of reading each groupette aloud, item by item, again and again. Then test yourself by writing the groupette's items to see if you have learned what you are reading. Be sure to relearn any groupette which gives you trouble.

Another technique for learning a topic is to teach it to another person. Haven't you found that if you teach anyone anything you learn it more thoroughly yourself? To teach, you really have to take a topic apart, divide it into smaller segments, present it in this form, and put it together again. This almost always assures you of understanding the subject. It points out any areas which are missing.

Still another technique for studying is to work with another person and to question each other. This, too, is excellent, because it involves constantly questioning and, therefore, thinking to formulate responses.

The methods we have just outlined will work in almost all circumstances, providing you have a body of material which you must make part of your storehouse of knowledge.

How to Avoid Wasting Time

We have seen classes playing cards. ("Our regular teacher is absent," the children tell us. "Their teacher didn't leave any work," the substitute proclaims.) We've seen them playing records and dancing. We've seen them playing games. All of these activities sound horrendous, and yet they can be used constructively. When? They can be used as rewards when assigned work is completed or after a big test to relieve the tension. They can be used as part of a party, and we feel that parties have a very definite place in the classroom. But we also know that there is much time wasted because of a lack of planning and organization on the part of the teacher.

Plan for every minute of every day, and then add material for an extra 25%. You'll find that you never run out of worthwhile material if you plan in this manner.

One of the easier ways to plan that extra time is to plan to use it for vocabulary development. Your average child needs this. He or she needs to know many words in order to be able to communicate.

Use 5 X 7 index cards. Select topics, and have a list of eight to ten words on each card. When the class has completed the work they have been doing, each child may select one card. On the card you may have one of a number of different assignments for each list of words. Here are some suggestions:

1. Alphabetize the words and figure out why they are grouped together on the card. (For example, the following words might be placed on one card: saute, boil, poach, simmer, broil, roast, steam, fry. These are all methods of cooking food.)
2. State the meaning of each word in your own words. (Don't copy from the dictionary.)
3. Look up the meaning of each word in the dictionary. Copy that definition.
4. Use the word in a sentence.
5. Write a paragraph using all of the words.

6. Draw a sketch to illustrate each word.
7. Give the part of speech of each word.
8. Write a funny sentence using each word.

Your groups of words can deal with food, clothing, shelter, careers, sports, tools, music, art, architecture, toys, astronomy, or almost any subject on earth. Try to develop lists of other parts of speech in addition to nouns, which are, of course, the simplest to develop.

This type of work is essential for the development of every person. Furthermore, since vocabulary is tested as part of both reading and intelligence, your children will truly benefit from this type of teaching.

Use every minute of every day. If you have a feeling of urgency, your children will too. If you don't appear to be pressured, they'll take it easy too.

One teacher has a huge sign across the front of her room: MINDS AT WORK—ALL THE TIME. Don't you agree that that's the way it should be?

How to Use Expectations to
Raise Achievement Levels

One of the most important aspects of raising achievement levels is the teacher's attitude. What is your expectation of the work your children are capable of doing? Many children have never been told, never been given any indication of the caliber of work they are capable of doing.

At the beginning of the year, tell your children: "I'd like to give each of you an A (or a 90 or whatever you use to indicate excellent work). You have it to begin with. Now you'll have to work to keep it." Then go on to explain your requirements. Be very specific. When the first marking period is over, show the child exactly what he or she has done. Indicate in what areas he or she can and should do better. Judge what each is capable of and then work with him or her to reach that goal. Set reasonable goals, of course, but then be sure that they are reached.

If, even in your own mind, you think, "They'll never do *that*," change *that* to something they can do—and expect them to do it.

The average child needs your expectation of him or her to be high. The lower it is, the less he or she will learn. This has been shown experimentally many times.

The opposite approach has the expected results too. Tell your children that they're poor students, and they will be. It isn't nearly as encouraging when a teacher acts surprised at the good work youngsters do as when he or she says, "I expected it all along." In the former case, the child thinks, "Maybe I'm not as dumb as the teacher thinks I am." In the latter, the reaction is, "That teacher thinks I'm smart."

You can help your average children fulfill your expectations. Follow these steps:

1. Teach them material you feel they must learn.
2. Explain the material carefully and as fully as possible.
3. Give the class notes to study from and instruct them to study these notes.
4. Give an informal quiz to determine which aspects of the material they haven't learned.
5. Go over the material they haven't learned.
6. Retest.
7. If need be, teach the material again. If only a few children need this reteaching, give the rest of the class new material while those who need the review are getting it.
    a. Select for this type of teaching the material you feel every child must know.
    b. Almost refuse to take "I can't" for an answer. This philosophy will work for your average child. It may not work for your slow learners, but you'll find that it can be of great help to most of the youngsters in your class.

Chapter 2

How to Reach and Teach

the Slow Learner

In the previous chapter, a plan was outlined which we feel works very well for all children. In this chapter we'll apply it specifically to those youngsters who are slow learners. Let us include in this category any child who does not grasp material the first or second time you teach it. For our present purposes, this definition is adequate.

How to Use the Key—Diagnosis

To begin with, it is essential that you think through every topic you are teaching. Determine exactly:

1. What concepts and examples you expect every child in the class to learn.
2. Which material, exactly, you expect the average and bright children to master.
3. Which material, exactly, you expect only the bright children to master.

This does not mean that all of your slow learners will master only the minimum material. Many will learn more than that.

Many of the average learners will grasp some of the material you've prepared for the bright children. But in your plan decide what material is absolutely essential for every child, if he is at all capable of doing so, to learn. This is your foundation, your floor, your rock bottom. This is your basic curriculum.

Next teach the material, beginning with this basic curriculum and enriching it.

1. Use at least two different approaches or techniques. You may begin with a filmstrip and continue with a reading lesson in social studies. In science, an experiment may be followed by a discussion. In mathematics, a demonstration using real materials followed by problem-solving would be appropriate. The different approaches are important because if children do not learn certain material by one method they may be able to grasp it by another.

2. Give the class specific notes, showing exactly what you expect them to know. State the material for the slow learners in the first few items and then increase the difficulty of the items. You may even decide to tell your children, "This is the target for us for today. Try to learn it all." Then, privately, tell certain children, "Your targets are the first four items. Please concentrate on those and you'll pass the test."

3. Give the children instructions teaching them how to study. (Suggestions are included in the previous chapter.)

4. Test the children. It is most important that you include enough material of a simple nature so that your slow learners will be able to pass if they have studied.

5. Using the children's papers, diagnose where their errors are.

6. Reteach the material until the children learn it.

    a. You may use pupil tutors, your brighter or average students, to do this.

    b. You may use paraprofessionals.

c. You may reteach it yourself to the slow learners while your other pupils are doing work to reinforce this material. (Rexographed worksheets, workbooks, or projects are excellent for this.)

d. You may ask for parental assistance. (Do this only if you know that there is someone at home who can help. It is useless if you are not certain of this and can, possibly, do more harm than good.)

e. You may work with the slow learners during any unassigned time you wish to devote to this purpose. We have found that this type of individualization can be extremely effective.

How to Diagnose Each Child's Needs

You must be aware of where each child is in terms of the material you are teaching. We have observed, for example, that the concept of the sentence is a very difficult one for slow learners. They may be able to state the definition of a sentence, but rarely can they apply it in their writing. Therefore, give the children a topic on which their thoughts will flow. Have them write. Then, using their papers, study exactly what type of errors they are making. Try having them read their work aloud and correct it as they actually group the words together in their speech, although they did not do so on paper.

You can diagnose in many ways. Written tests are obvious. You see very quickly which material the child has failed to learn. This is fine providing you do not penalize the child because he is unable to read. Let us say that a slow learner has learned the concepts and facts you have taught but then doesn't understand the questions you've asked him or her to read as part of the test. To prevent this, and incidentally to avoid discouraging your slow learners, you can read the tests aloud, making sure that the youngsters understand the questions. This, we feel, is very fair to all of the children.

The ability to answer questions is also a skill—which should be taught. If your slow learners (and often the average and bright children can benefit from this type of instruction, too) need help in writing responses to questions, teach them how this should be done.

As teachers we have a tendency to take things for granted. Our vocabularies are often so large compared to those of our pupils that we have to be extremely careful to be sure that our slow learners understand what we are saying. We're reminded of the little boy who questioned his teacher when she said, "Dogs' homes are usually with families, but some dogs live in kennels."

The child looked incredulous. "How can a dog live in a kennel?" he asked. "They're so small."

"Kennels aren't small," the teacher said as she sketched one on the board. Now the child looked utterly bewildered. The teacher, sensing there was a problem, asked, "What kind of kennel are you thinking about?"

"The kind my mother puts water into when she wants to make tea," the child responded.

You will find that if you establish goals for your slow learners, discuss them with them, and work toward their solution, far more will be accomplished than if you have no specific objectives. You may call these goals behavioral objectives if you prefer, or goals, aims, or objectives. The name is not as important as having the goals. A goal such as "Pupil can answer simple questions by writing a correct response of one sentence to each" is very appropriate regardless of the grade you teach, because very often, even in high school, slow learners are unable to do this. Another behavioral objective, "Pupil will be able to sign his name legibly and write his address," is appropriate for many lower grade levels. Of course, many children will have no need for special help in this area, but for those slow learners who need it, it can be invaluable!

How to Teach Individually to Meet the Child's Needs

We recently met a teacher who said, "I had to flunk three-quarters of my freshman class. They wouldn't do the work I assigned. I warned them that's what would happen, and it did!"

"Why don't you begin your class with a unit on reproduction?" we asked. (This was a high school biology teacher to whom we were speaking). "They'd do better in that."

"Why should I? I'll fail the whole class if I have to."

This teacher's attitude is one of the horrors of our educational system. This teacher was totally oblivious to the needs of most of the members of the class. Our response was superficial and yet really quite relevant. At that age, young people are interested in reproduction and would probably be motivated to study this subject.

Our approach can't be heartless or dogmatic. If it is, what are we really doing? By individualizing your instruction, you can reach down to the nitty gritty. You can make learning relevant and vital.

You must begin, as was previously stated, by establishing exactly what it is you expect your slow learners to absorb, dividing the work into very small areas and then working on these areas until they do. This may not be easy to do, but it can be accomplished. How many children reach the fourth grade unable to read the words which make up the Dolch list? Often this is not because the teachers didn't try but because there was no zeroing in on individual aspects, no concentration on details. By teaching the whole and neglecting details, we sometimes fail to teach at all.

Let us use as an example teaching the forms of business letters in the seventh grade. Instead of teaching a whole letter, break it down into its elements and then teach each one.

The business letter consists of:

1. Heading
2. Inside address
3. Salutation
4. Body
5. Closing of the letter
6. Complimentary close
7. Signature

Having broken the letter down into these parts, establish a project for which children will want to write business letters. Teach them how to write the letters and then have them practice until each of the seven details is perfect. In this way, because it is relatively simple to check each detail, you can zero in on exactly where the learning problems are.

It is truly amazing how few young people are able to write appropriate business letters. This lesson will be useful all through junior and senior high school. Answering job advertisements is an excellent project for teaching letter writing. Your slow learners especially need this help for their future lives.

How to Group to Meet the Child's Needs

If you were to teach the example given above, you would probably find not one but a number of children who could not grasp the concept of the body of the letter. It is not necessary to teach them individually. Take a group of children who have made the same error and have them work on it together. You may wish to have them try to figure out by themselves where their problems are. This is more effective than your or any other person's telling them again and again.

To accomplish grouping, there are several steps to follow:

1. Make your groups fluid. Don't have any group last longer than the time it takes to achieve the particular objective. By following this rule, you will be able to avoid stigmatizing any child.

2. Don't put disruptive children in the same group if you can help it. This will prevent the entire group from working, which is unfair to the other children. *When you find that you have created a disruptive group, break it up immediately!*

3. Groups may consist of two or three children or contain as many as eight to twelve children. That's about the largest group that we've found is able to work together. If you experiment and find otherwise, of course use whichever size you find effective.

If you have paraprofessionals who can teach the group, give them specific instructions as to what material you want covered. You may use student helpers, too.

4. Whenever you do group work, be sure that each group has work to do. There is an inclination for children to play. If *you*

change the work into play by the method you use, that's great. If *the children* turn it into play, that's trouble.

As an example of group work, let's say that a group is working on the concept, "In the body of a business letter you must state the reason for writing the letter in the first sentence." Ask the group to suggest possible first sentences, being as humorous or unusual—but grammatically correct—as possible.

We saw one boy write, perfectly correctly, "I am writing to ask your company if you would take volunteers to be part of your space program." To say the least, NASA would find such a request interesting. Children enjoy being funny—and will try to be so within the framework you suggest.

"I am writing this letter to ask if you could send me some old dollar bills. I read you burned them," another child wrote to the Bureau of Printing and Engraving.

One girl's letter began in a different vein. "Dear Santa," she wrote, "This is the first time I've ever written to you correctly."

5. As soon as the reason for the group's existence is over, break it up! Don't even give it a name. Too often children will be aware of what the groupings mean. "I'm in the bluebirds," a child once told me. "They're the do-do birds." He then added, "Do-do birds are dumb!" This stigmatizing should never be done to any child, even temporarily. Every youngster's ego is fragile, and self-esteem is essential.

6. Be sure that you group children according to areas in which each child at one time or another can excel. We've seen non-academically talented boys teaching basketball skills to their academically brighter classmates with great success.

How to Build on Previous Strength and Knowledge

Every child has strength and knowledge in some area—academic or non-academic. Building on that strength can make a vast difference, because it supplies you with at least a small ego structure with which to work.

For example, many boys are involved in sports. If you are teaching arithmetic, it is as easy to bring in examples from the sports world as from any other. Instead of having arithmetic problems dealing with shopping all the time, vary your examples.

"Sam Smith is a great home run hitter. If he hit six homers in his last three games, and two were in the first game, how many were in the other games?"

The same is true of reading. If you want to develop a facility in reading, why not begin with the newspaper—even if the pupils are unable to grasp every word? In fact, from the articles they read (which you can have them clip out and paste into their notebooks) have them select the words to be studied in their vocabulary development work. Reading the newspaper is a skill they will need and use repeatedly. Why not teach them early?

What if your pupils aren't involved in sports? Find out in your conferences what they are involved in, or you can determine interests from class discussions. You should be able to find some area in which each child has already accumulated knowledge. Use that as a starting point. Don't ignore baseball cards, movie stars, and horses.

These strengths can be used for all the communication skills—for reading, writing, and speaking and listening. They can be used as the basis for art and other creative work, too.

How about monsters, television, music, stamps, or dogs and other pets? One highly successful teacher taught a full unit on embryology beginning with the incubation and the hatching of ducks in her classroom. The children all developed a deep interest in the subject as a result, and many pursued this interest.

How to Develop Vocabulary in Every Subject Area

We have already covered one technique for the development of vocabulary in every subject area. Here is another; it is called "The Vocabulary Sweepstakes."

At the beginning of the term have each child bring in ten words on a particular topic. You may allow the youngsters to select their own topics, or you can assign them. The words can be selected from any subject area you feel needs vocabulary development.

Have each word printed on a 3 X 5 index card, with one dictionary meaning if your class is on the fifth grade level or below. If your class is on the sixth grade level, require each word to have at least two meanings. On the reverse side of the index card, have the children place their names.

Compile a list of words, and each day have the class learn five of them. (In about three months all of the words will have been covered.) They should be written on the board under the title "Vocabulary Sweepstakes."

After all of the words have been analyzed by studying the spelling, writing definitions, using them in sentences, and then using them in compositions, you must determine the class winners. One set of winners should be the youngsters who have learned the most words, as revealed on a written test or in a vocabulary bee (held as you'd hold a spelling bee). Another set of winners might be the youngsters able to use the most words in a composition. (Warning: It's not fair to write, "I have to use as many of the following words in a composition as I can," followed by a list of the words.) Still another set of winners should be those pupils whose words were most remembered. This can be determined by using the same test mentioned above.

Books and dictionaries are very appropriate prizes. If there is any way you can have the youngsters select their own, they would probably enjoy it. Sample copies of books are sometimes available from your supervisor.

Vocabulary development through the sweepstakes is an ongoing program, carried on as a game. Always try to make learning fun. This is one simple way of doing so.

How to Cope with Mental Blocks

Have you ever observed a person trying to communicate with an individual who is unable to speak the same language? Often the first person speaks slowly. Then he tries to speak more clearly. His tone often gets louder and louder. The other person is rarely if ever any closer to understanding. But then the speaker may make gestures. Aha! Some recognition results! Or the speaker may actually physically move the other one in a given direction. Or he may look for someone who speaks the other person's language. So it is with teaching. Speaking more slowly, clearly, or loudly doesn't really help nearly as much as finding other methods. Finding other methods often requires rethinking an entire subject.

If a slow learner in your class can't grasp a topic, try a completely different approach from the one you've taken before. If you've been using verbal methods, change them to written ones. If the text you're using is not right, replace it with another. Try new workbooks or duplicated materials.

It is not as important to find out why a child is blocked as it is to help him or her to break that pattern. If he or she is made to feel, or allowed to feel, stupid, there may be very serious consequences. Treat the block lightly, saying, "Let's try this another way," or "We can use this worksheet today." Children are tremendously sensitive to criticism, especially the slow learners.

How to Develop Self-Esteem
and Self-Confidence

Several months ago, we were told that one of our eighth graders should be in a class for retarded children. The child is emotionally disturbed. She is hyperenergetic and cannot sit in a seat and listen for more than five minutes. She therefore has a tendency to ask for a pass and roam the halls.

"Beating her doesn't help," her mother told me. "She cries, says she'll behave, and then does the same thing over and over again."

However, she is by no means retarded. An eighth grader, she scored 2.5 on a reading test. Her teacher protested. "She's not nearly that poor a reader," he insisted. "She's reading seventh and eighth grade SRA material. She can't be reading at a 2.5 level." Sure enough, upon investigation, we discovered that she got up before the test "to take a drink of water." When she sat down she moved her answer paper so that it was not correctly lined up, and all the little boxes were in the wrong place. So were all the answers.

A subsequent test resulted in a score of 6.6. However, our reason for telling this story is to point out the effect that the announcement, "You should be in the retarded class," had on the child. To begin with, she should never have been told. How it "got out" is a mystery. Her reaction was sheer fury. "I know I'm bad," she said, "but I'm not retarded." Even telling her, "We know you aren't retarded, and you aren't even bad. You never hurt another child. You just can't sit still," couldn't reassure her. Then the 2.5 on the test! But her reaction was, "Let me read to you. I can read. I know I can!" And, of course, she can.

The 6.6 score? Well, the comment this little girl made was the clincher: "I thought I could do it, but until I could show you, what difference did it make?"

We have to give the slow learners opportunities to show us, because in showing us they are showing themselves. Brighter children have chances to do this often. Our slow learners need to have their chances structured. How can we do this?

Are your children given standardized reading tests? If so, prepare material of the same type and have them practice with it. (In some school systems it's permissible to use old tests. If you can, do so by all means; if not, compose your own.)

Do the same for helping them with the material on which they will be tested for reading comprehension. You can take newspaper articles, for example, and adapt them. Or you can take paragraphs from magazines or books. Sometimes even the work written by some of the students of the class can be adapted. Then, using the test as a guide, write your own questions. Often these involve the following:

1. The main idea (usually phrased as: "What would be the best title for this paragraph?")
2. Word meanings based on the use of the word in the selection; e.g., "There are *great* states and small states in our nation." (What does "great" mean in this sentence?)
3. Making references: "Many people feel that the earth is in a state of flux. One of the most active areas rings the Pacific Ocean." (The question might be, "Which of the

following might occur in Japan?" a. a monsoon, b. a tidal wave, c. an unusually cold winter, or d. a famine.)

We have found that our students enjoy doing worksheets with this type of material. They can correct the sheets themselves or exchange papers. This work helps them to do better on standardized tests than they would without such practice.

How to Build a Success Pattern

You will find that your slow learners will respond positively to the type of work which makes them feel that they are "on top" of the situation.

Here are a number of ways to give them this feeling:

Give each pupil some responsibility which he or she can handle. If you observe that he or she isn't doing a good job, without berating him or her, change the task. Distributors of papers, collectors of papers, class librarians, gardeners, printers, photographers, tutors, artists, athletes. The list of tasks you can develop is endless. However, if you see that the task doesn't suit the child, change it.

Use the following method of preparing your children for tests. Then post your tests on the bulletin boards. Cover the room with them.

1. Select material the slow learners are capable of mastering.

2. If need be, give individual assignments or group assignments, but vary them so that they don't appear to be geared for slower children.

3. Teach the material using several methods.

4. Have the children do written work, reviewing until they can complete the assignment perfectly.

5. Then, and only then, test them. When each child gets 100%, your work is completed. Post the papers on the bulletin board. When you have a new set of papers to display, return the old papers to the children.

Have each child keep a portfolio and place this work in it. Give other work which the child can do successfully. Include creative work as well. Many slow learners can design planes, cars, and the like. Include these in the portfolios and post them.

Create a spirit of freedom and inquiry in your class. Encourage your children to bring in things of interest. Give credit for all contributions. Be lavish with praise and with grades. It is astounding to see how children grow and flower in this type of positive environment.

Chapter 3

How to Get the Maximum Achievement
from Your Intellectually Gifted Students

Of late it seems that the intellectually gifted students have become the "forgotten men" (and women) of our classrooms. There has been an inordinate amount of pressure to teach every child to read (which, we hasten to add, is surely justified), but it should not be at the expense of the more capable youngsters. We have seen many bright youngsters become bored and disinterested. A vicious cycle is born. They're bored, so they don't do their work. Their teachers will reprimand them—the kids call it hassling—and, as a result, they get "turned off." Gifted children are the ones who need and search for stimulation. We know that when they reach adolescence they will sometimes look for it in drugs—because of peer group pressure or because of what was originally wholesome curiosity. (We once previewed a filmstrip about drugs and understood for the first time how this happens. The illustrations of what a trip on LSD was like were so interesting that every adult present at the screening agreed that his or her curiosity was aroused.)

Many intellectually gifted children are physically more mature than their classmates, and that, too, should be taken into consideration. When they are not challenged, they often seek older companions and other sources of stimulation.

We have found that bright children need enrichment and responsibility. They must be overworked, rather than underworked. (We have dealt, over the many years we have been in the school system as teacher, counselor, and administrator, with thousands of parents. On only two occasions was the charge made, "My child is being overworked." Hundreds of times it was just the opposite. "The trouble is my son never has any work to do." "Doesn't my daughter ever get a book she must read?" "Don't the children have homework sometimes?" Even the answer, "They do, and they do it during their lunch hour," is not very satisfying.)

The intellectually gifted child, because he or she is rarely a discipline problem, is often not given his or her share of attention in the classroom. He or she deserves better! It is the purpose of this chapter to show you how to enrich your program so that these youngsters will benefit greatly from your teaching. This is one of those wonderful situations from which everyone benefits. Parents are delighted, and the public relations aspect is great. All of the children in the class (all—not just the bright) will come out way ahead, and you will find your teaching far more enjoyable and stimulating for you.

How to Present New Material

Your intellectually gifted children will usually grasp the material you are teaching relatively quickly. They will learn most of it, if not all of it, with relatively little effort. They'll go through the written assignments in record time. It's after they have completed their regular work that the enrichment process should begin.

It isn't fair for any child to have to sit through three or four lessons on a topic which he learned the first time or even knew before you began teaching it. (Incidentally, the use of pre- and post-tests for this purpose is very important. If any child has not learned what you are teaching, he or she should not go on to new material. We have found that many bright children have not learned fundamental writing skills. They can discuss any subject—indeed, their verbal skills are excellent. But verbal skills do not fulfill the need to use written language correctly. There are many colleges which have had to institute remedial writing courses because their students were so lacking in written communication skills.)

Present any subject you are teaching. Give a pre-test. Then base your teaching on the results. Next, give a post-test. Every child who needs reteaching should get it. Every child who has mastered the material should be given new material.

Let us assume that your bright children have completed their regular work. You can use a number of devices to teach new material to them.

1. Creation of original material
2. Preparation of oral presentations
3. Research projects on related subjects

These are three basic types of assignments which will enable you to present new material so that it is thought-provoking and challenging.

Make no mistake—if you offer "busy work," your bright children may or may not do it, but it will in no way enrich the curriculum the way solid additions would.

Let us study how to make these new materials "solid."

1. Creation of original material

Your class is working on the New England states. They have been studying the history and geography of the area. After the intellectually gifted have learned the basics, what can they do?

a. Design a game which could cover geographical or historical facts related to New England.
b. Design a menu using food of that region. Gather and study recipes; convert the recipes to the amounts to be used to prepare the food for the entire class. Then actually prepare the meal.
c. Work up a mural depicting the history.
d. Make a collage showing famous historic places of the area.
e. Design a sign containing as many symbols of the area as possible. (Bean pot, lantern, teapot, ship, and so on.)

    f. Plan a trip by car through all of the famous places, indicating routes, stops, and reasons for making those stops.

    g. Prepare a moving pictorial description of the area. Put this on rollers. Pictures should be of uniform size. Paste them on a long sheet, arranged so that each picture may be viewed by itself.

2. Preparation of oral presentations

    a. Teach a lesson. Allow pupil to select a topic he or she would like to teach. Discuss the parts of a lesson and allow students to prepare and teach it. You may also use a mini-lesson, depending on the amount of material the student wants to cover.

    b. Debates can be a very exciting and stimulating device. However, beware! Debates need structure. We've seen bright students give poor debates because of lack of structure.

To prepare a debate, students should work together. They should know exactly what they are debating and prepare their arguments.

We recently observed a debate on "Women's Lib." Certainly the topic has gotten widespread publicity. It should have led to an excellent debate—but it didn't for the following reasons:

1. The students involved had no clear idea of what they were debating. A topic such as "Woman's place is in the home" would have sufficed. *A clear statement of topic is essential.*

2. They had some facts, but they were all on one topic. They concentrated on Susan B. Anthony and woman's suffrage but on nothing else. Yet they were not debating women having the right to vote. Facts supporting the basic premise were needed.

3. There was no rebuttal. Implicit in a debate is the concept that there are two sides to it. The members of the other team had nothing prepared.

Debates need careful preparation. Teach your children how to select topics and then how to prepare the debates step by step. Teach them how to make points and prepare the rebuttal.

 c. Prepare a campaign of some sort—for a possible political candidate, for a community betterment program, or on a problem of worldwide significance.

 d. Prepare "radio" or "television" programs to be presented to the class.

 e. Research and plan a class trip.

3. Research projects on related subjects

Research can be fascinating providing it is on a stimulating topic. Your challenge is to supply these topics. We've found that gifted children will respond to them. For example:

 a. The world population will reach four billion within your lifetime. Where will the food come from to feed all of these people?

 b. Much of our country is wasteland. What can be done about this?

 c. The railroads are in great financial trouble, and yet our nation needs them. What can be done to help them?

 d. Alaska is now being developed. What is being done there? Are the crimes which were committed against the Indians being repeated?

 e. How has our government changed in the 200 years of its existence?

 f. We have observed that most gifted children enjoy doing research on the lives of people with whom they can identify. A careful choice will often pay big dividends. If you have them research the lives of living people, correspondence with these persons can add to the interest.

How to Utilize the Talents of
the Intellectually Gifted Child

1.   All of the projects outlined above may be used to teach the entire class. When you use this approach, however, be sure that you check the work of each child before allowing him or her to present it to the class. Many times, children (even gifted ones) will not do a complete job—and it is up to the teacher to ascertain whether or not the job is complete before the project is presented to the rest of the class.

One of the most successful lessons we have observed students teaching was based on "The Four Food Groups." The fifth graders had been studying nutrition; the gifted ones created a game. It used Monopoly as the basic structure, with tasks to be done (related to nutrition) in order to advance around the board. Nutrients, calories, vitamins, and minerals were all taken into consideration and worked into the game plan. (The idea for basing a game on this topic came from a government-published game called "The Four Food Groups for Better Meals Game," available for $3.95 from the Government Printing Office.)

2.   In many classes the gifted children tutor other children in the class. This can be used on occasion to stimulate the bright children.

3.   Tutoring children in the lower grades. Probably the most effective tutoring is on an individual basis. However, we have seen fifth graders tutor groups and sixth graders teach entire classes.

If tutoring is to be successful, the tutors must be given very explicit instructions. It is not enough for the teacher to say, "Read this story and ask Johnny questions about it." The tutor should be told exactly what questions to ask and what the other pupil's response should be.

If a teacher wants to use gifted children to tutor youngsters in his or her class, he or she should have a briefing session and frequent conferences with them in much the same way as a teacher works with paraprofessionals.

Parental permission should be obtained if any youngster does tutoring. We have seen parents object because they had not been informed. Most youngsters who do the tutoring benefit from the activity. It gives them poise and a chance to do something worthwhile for another human being. This development of "caring" can carry over into all aspects of living. Many tutors are pupils interested in becoming teachers, and tutoring gives them a chance to sample the profession.

4.   Many gifted children can find an outlet in writing. There are many suitable projects, among which are the following:

    (a)   Keeping a journal. This is a book in which the children write their ideas, their aspirations, their delights, and their disappointments. It differs from a diary, which is usually more of a chronicle of events.

    (b)   Writing skits and plays. Children love satire, and they are usually anxious to satirize anything. Television commercials are a good place to begin. Ask the children to prepare their own—and watch the fun!

5.   Bright children have prepared excellent assembly programs. Quiz shows are a particular favorite. They can model them on quiz shows from television. We saw one production in which "fabulous" prizes were given away—pictures of the prizes, that is. The audience appreciated the gimmick and really got into the spirit of it.

6.   A newspaper or magazine is an excellent project for bright children to work on. If the paper or magazine is to represent the work of a small group rather than the entire class, give the group a name and refer to it that way. One such group of pupils in a fifth grade class produced a wonderful series of children's books. The group called itself "The Seven Dwarfs."

7.   Community projects are another area in which bright children can become involved. In one area of our community a group of pupils did a survey. They uncovered the fact that there was a severe lack of litter baskets in a huge part of our borough, including a lovely park, which, because of this lack, was becoming unattractive. When called to the attention of the Department of Sanitation, the situation was remedied.

How to Avoid Wasting the Time
of the Gifted Child

1. As you plan your lessons, you must decide which activities you will offer to your bright children. List four or five in your plan. Don't offer too many, because that makes the decision too difficult and often requires the youngsters to take too much time to consider.

2. One very successful teacher offered a mini-course, available to every pupil who completed his or her work. She began with one in pottery making. The children were only moderately enthusiastic. Photography proved a much more attractive topic.

3. There is no reason why children should not be permitted to read when they have completed their classwork. Indeed, we believe that they should be encouraged to do so. However, for this activity books should be selected from the class library. The class library should be liberally stocked with books that are just slightly above the children's reading level. Here is a chance to introduce authors such as Rafael Sabatini and Mark Twain, whom children might not choose on their own.

How to Have Your Bright Children Do
People-to-People Research

Children can do amazing research if you are willing to take the time to teach them how. It is necessary, though, that they see the value in their work and the reason for doing it.

Our community contains Sailor's Snug Harbor, a residence for retired seamen which was established by a sea captain many years ago. One group of bright seventh graders, who were doing research on folk music, had an unforgettable experience when they interviewed an 80-year-old sailor as part of their project. Fortunately, they tape-recorded his responses.

Another interest-provoking type of research is into various career areas. Again, one of the best techniques is interviewing. It is an excellent technique when it is combined with visits to on-the-spot locations.

Research into the reasons immigrants left (or leave) their native lands to come here can prove very interesting. Many immigrants come to our shores each year.

There is really no limit to the topics you can develop. One social studies class of sixth graders made candles based on the research done by several of the youngsters in the class as part of a bicentennial celebration.

In order to be successful:

1. Help the gifted children to select topics of high interest value.

2. Cover with them exactly what they are trying to find out.

3. Give them a start by suggesting where they can find information.

4. In some way, make use of the material they develop.

One of the huge areas which can really challenge gifted children is "How does it work?" The question may refer to a telephone, a zipper, an elevator, or a computer. There are so many things we use daily which are beyond the comprehension of most adults. It can be a source of great satisfaction for a youngster when he is asked at the dinner table what he learned in school that day to be able to answer, "I found out how a radio works. Want to know how?"

Intellectually gifted children are often the ones who become concerned about world, national, and local problems. This concern can be utilized as the basis for research. Environmental concerns, because they are often in the news, can provide stimulating projects.

How to Use Problem-Solving as an Instructional Technique

In our lifetimes each of us has many and varied problems to solve. Intellectually gifted children often go into career areas which involve constant problem solving. Engineering comes to mind immediately. If we train our students to use problem-solving techniques, we can give them tools that they will use all their lives.

The basic "scientific method" of reasoning—determine what the problem is, figure out a possible solution, test it, if that is not the solution try another approach, and keep trying until you find one which works—can be used by gifted children in many ways.

Edison used exactly this method to determine the filament best suited for electric light bulbs, and he tested over a thousand different materials.

Most often the problems solved are scientific in nature. "How can we grow larger-than-average vegetables" was one problem that we attempted to solve. The students experimented with a variety of fertilizers.

Another area is health learnings. Several gifted children were anxious to find out if a person's diet had an effect on whether his or her skin broke out. They devised a questionnaire (Figure 3-1) and asked many of their schoolmates to fill it out. You may wish to use it with your class.

---

1. Does your skin break out with many pimples often? (Many is more than 10 at one time.)
   Often_____ Sometimes_____ Rarely_____ Never_____
2. Do you eat vegetables?
   Often_____ Sometimes_____ Rarely_____ Never_____
3. Do you eat chocolate or drink chocolate milk three times a week?
   Often_____ Sometimes_____ Rarely_____ Never_____
4. Do you eat pizza three times a week?
   Often_____ Sometimes_____ Rarely_____ Never_____
5. Do you eat French fried potatoes three times a week?
   Often_____ Sometimes_____ Rarely_____ Never_____
6. Do you eat fruit?
   Often_____ Sometimes_____ Rarely_____ Never_____
7. Do you eat bacon?
   Often_____ Sometimes_____ Rarely_____ Never_____
8. Do you eat ice cream?
   Often_____ Sometimes_____ Rarely_____ Never_____

Figure 3-1

From the results of the responses to the questionnaire, they were able to conclude the following:

1. There were some people who ate all of the items listed and never had pimples.
2. There were some people who ate all of the items and had many pimples.
3. More of the people who ate fatty foods often had pimples.

They enjoyed working with the questionnaire and realized the difficulties involved in drawing conclusions.

Construction problems are often a challenge to intellectually gifted students. For example, one class was preparing to work on a project which required an incubator. The gifted children experimented until they found the right size bulb and developed a means of humidifying the box after they were able to keep the temperature constant. (Note: This project can end in disaster if the temperature goes up too high.)

How to Develop Leadership Qualities

We have observed time and again that children can develop leadership qualities. Intellectually gifted children often blossom in this regard, and development of leadership qualities can be very important if they are shy or reticent. To foster this development, one of the key words is responsibility. Given responsibility, and being advised of it, many children will rise to the occasion.

We have asked gifted children to actually counsel younger children. This has proved successful in the settling of many differences. We have found that an excellent spirit of responsibility and leadership developed when an older child began to look after the younger ones.

By giving gifted children responsibility in such areas as the collection of money and record keeping we help them learn how to conduct themselves. (Payments for milk or for a trip are examples of money the children can collect.)

Buzz Groups

Buzz groups are another technique for developing leadership. Divide the class into groups of five or six students and assign one of your gifted children to lead the group. Give the group an assignment to do and put a time limit on it.

Assignments may consist of topics to be discussed; e.g., "How can our class behavior be improved?" "How can I get more benefit from school?" Questions on social mores such as "What time should people our age be required to come home?" or "What is one way to make new friends?" usually lead to good discussions.

Another way to use buzz groups is to give an academic assignment such as "Describe the treatment of the Indians in North Carolina," or "Develop a paragraph containing six verbs beginning with the letters 'a,' 'b,' and 'c,' and three nouns with the letters 'r,' 's,' and 't' in them."

Through buzz groups, gifted children get the experience of leading a group. They learn firsthand how difficult it is to keep a group on target.

Debates and teaching situations also foster the development of leadership qualities. The same is true of the use of class officers elected by the students.

Academic achievement should be rewarded. If your school has an "Honor Roll," any child who earns a place on it should see his or her name recorded. Other achievements—in sports, music, school service, community service—should also be noted on special charts or lists.

How to Prevent the Gifted Child from Developing a "Swelled Head"

We all know people who are obnoxious because of their inflated opinions of themselves. This can easily happen to gifted children. In order to prevent this problem, teachers should find a way to include every child in an honor list. (Every child can do school service—providing you give him or her the opportunity to do so.)

Many intellectually gifted children escape the "swelled head" syndrome, but there are almost invariably some who don't. It is critical to the lives of the latter that they learn to accept their gifts and to use them wisely rather than flaunting them at the expense of others.

Children who exhibit arrogant behavior often are ostracized by the other youngsters in the class, and this can make them extremely unhappy. To prevent this from happening, handle the problem as soon as you can. If you see a child being unpleasant, discuss it with him or her immediately.

Encourage give-and-take on the part of *every* child. It's so easy to call on the volunteers—usually the gifted children—and virtually to ignore the others. We've seen teachers who are guilty of this and are completely unaware of what they are doing. Other teachers ignore the gifted children.

How to Encourage the Bright Child
to Plan for Future Education and Career Development

Intellectually gifted children in your classes need and deserve to be inspired and encouraged to aim high when they think of career preparation.

Some months ago, we received a letter from a young lady who was about to graduate from the eighth grade and go on to high school. She had been an excellent student. She mentioned in her letter that she planned to become a laboratory technician. We made an appointment to speak to her and asked if she were really interested in becoming a technician or if she really wanted a career involved with health. She thought for a short time and then said "Health."

"Why not become a doctor?" we asked. Her answer was unbelievable.

"I never even thought of that. Would I be able to make it?" This girl had been a truly outstanding student. We hastened to assure her that she ought to think about it. She returned to show us her first report from high school. No grade was below 95.

As teachers we often take it for granted that our children have appropriate aspirations. We suggest that you use the questionnaire in Figure 3-2 to give you some idea of your students' thinking.

A review of the children's responses will give you some ideas in regard to their aspirations.

Aspirations

1. What is your favorite subject?
2. What is your favorite pastime?
3. Which adult do you know whom you would want to be like when you're an adult? Why?
4. If you could have any career in the world you wanted, what would it be? Why?
5. What education do you think a person needs for that career?
6. What job or career do you think you will have eventually? Why?
7. What education will you require for it?
8. What other career do you think might make you happy?

Figure 3-2

If your gifted children are to aim high, they must have some familiarity with career possibilities. *The Occupational Outlook for College Graduates* (1974-75 Edition) is published by the U.S. Department of Labor, Bureau of Labor Statistics, and sold for $2.95. It contains a variety of career descriptions. By using this book, you can base some of the work your gifted children do on careers in which they might be interested. You can, for instance, encourage them to investigate some of the careers described in this volume.

Trips to places of employment, speakers, films, or filmstrips are all excellent techniques for developing career awareness. Try to familiarize your students with professions about which they know relatively little. They probably know about teaching, medicine, dentistry, law, and engineering, but know comparatively little about other professions. Yet, in regard to number of men employed, accounting is second only to engineering. We have found that most young people are almost totally unaware of the career opportunities business offers.

It is important, too, to develop self-awareness. Many gifted children are not aware of their capabilities, and showing them their records may be the first step in this process. As is often the case, your children may never have seen their cumulative records and probably have never even thought of their potential.

No child should ever be discouraged. Children's academic performances may change; they often do. However, academic records provide a good basis for prediction of future academic work, and the chances are good that your gifted students will remain gifted throughout their academic careers. Isn't it up to us to encourage them to live and work up to their potential?

Chapter 4

How to Deal with Children
Who Have Problems Learning to Read

It is one of our beliefs that many behavioral problems are caused by one of two basic factors. Either the youngster misbehaves because he or she is psychologically disturbed, seriously (on a long-term basis) or temporarily (on a short-term basis), or that youngster cannot or has not learned to read.

We will deal at length with the problems of the psychologically disturbed child in later chapters. In this chapter we will address ourselves to the problem of the child who can't read.

The magnitude of the effects of an inability to read cannot be over-estimated. They are tremendous, and so far-reaching that they may hound a person for many years after he or she reaches maturity. The feelings of frustration and the destruction of self-confidence engendered by constant failure in this area have caused untold numbers of students to drop out of school— psychologically at the age of ten or twelve and physically at the age of sixteen, or whenever they were legally permitted to do so.

Recently, we worked with Betty Sue, a 13 year old who had been adjudged a school phobic. She had not attended school but had been given home instruction for five years; now the time had come for her to be returned to school. She appeared to be quite intelligent and had been taking first one and then two courses at our school. She also served as my office monitor, and we had become quite close. One day she confided, "I can't read."

I responded, "Oh, come on! I'm sure you can."

"No," she said, "I really can't."

"I have an idea," I said. I gave her a copy of *Jaws,* a best seller which moved the reader along very quickly because of the action of the story. I told her, "This book is so interesting you'll love it. It will carry you along. If you can't read a word or two, don't quit or get discouraged."

"But I can't read," Betty repeated.

"Just try," I begged. "Please give yourself a chance." I honestly was convinced that Betty could read if she attempted it.

"Okay, but I don't think so."

The next day, the child returned the book to me. "I knew I couldn't read it—and I couldn't," she said almost triumphantly.

"Did you really try?" I kept at it.

"Yes, I really did."

"Show me," I said, and opened the book. I still blush thinking about it. How could I have so embarrassed this poor child? How could I have put her through that torture? I guess (by way of apology) that I had found Betty so intelligent, so capable of doing the varied and difficult tasks I had assigned to her that I couldn't accept the fact that she really was unable to read.

Betty Sue read three words aloud correctly. The fourth one stumped her completely. I said it for her, and she read four more and then burst into tears. No amount of encouragement could help that child to read. Telling her she could was, I suddenly realized, the worst thing in the world. She *knew* she couldn't.

I am sure my reader joins me in blushing, because we know that there are so many Betty Sues in our country—and in the world. However, the plans which follow did help this particular child—and others like her.

Motivating the Child with Reading Problems

Begin by giving assurance to any child in your class who is having difficulty reading. "We will be using many methods and different techniques. Some of them will surely help you because they have helped many others." Discuss this concept, and then go on to the next point. "Think of the ability to read as a door which will open up a huge world of knowledge and pleasure to you." (Be sure that the children understand the meanings of the words "knowledge" and "pleasure.") "You are looking for the keys. We'll do all we can to help you. This door has many locks which take time to open, so you shouldn't become discouraged. There are many people who have had to make this same search." (This is very important. We've discovered that children don't realize others have the same problems they do. When they become aware that others have the same problems, their whole attitude changes. During the adolescent years, and, to a lesser degree, throughout childhood, children dread being considered different (or "freaks" as they may call it).

Don't hesitate to say, "You have a reading problem, but, by working together, I know that we can solve it." Also, say to any child with this problem, "If you have a question, never hesitate to ask me. If you don't understand, someone else doesn't either. You help me by asking questions. If I use a word that you don't understand, ask me to tell you the meaning or to spell it so that you can look up the definition in the dictionary. Knowing the meanings for words is a very important part of reading."

Repeat, and it cannot be said too often, "You can learn to read. We'll work together, but the responsibility is yours. You are, I know, mature enough to handle it." Use the word "mature" even with young children. It has been our experience that this is the greatest compliment you can pay them. (Again, make sure that they understand the definition of "mature.") We're really not sure of the reason, but this approach works. We're positive; we've used it innumerable times.

Now let us proceed with our strategies. We will begin with the Dolch list.

How to Use the Dolch List—Key One

The Dolch list is a list of those words which are encountered most frequently in any type of reading material. Copyright laws prohibit our reprinting the list, but it is available in every library.

Begin by working on this list. If the child with whom you are working cannot read every word, prepare a "hand card game" for him or her to use. Three-by-five index cards are fine for this purpose. Print one word from the Dolch list on one side of each card. (The child you are helping can do this, or another child may do the printing.) Then have the youngster read the words to another person. Remove the card of each word read correctly. If a word is read incorrectly, the card remains in the deck. The child "plays" until all the cards are removed. The child actually learns to recognize the words on sight by playing this game.

This game can be played by one child with a person checking him or her. It can also be played by two or more youngsters. In this case, the players take turns. After each turn, count the number of cards still left. These are considered as points, one point per card. The game ends when each player has gone out. The one with the lowest number of points wins.

In the case of the Dolch list, it is essential that the child with a reading problem learn all the words, no matter how long this takes. This is one of the keys—just one, but an important one.

Since learning the words on the Dolch list is so important, use any help you can get to assist the child. Parents, older siblings, paraprofessionals, even other students can work with the child who needs assistance. A letter home to the parents, or a phone call, is certainly worthwhile. Explain what you are trying to accomplish with the youngster and ask for cooperation. It is almost always forthcoming—if at all possible.

How to Use Diagnosis to Determine Where Difficulties Lie—Key Two

In dealing with problems, unless you determine exactly where they are, you will be working in the dark. How can you accomplish the necessary diagnosis?

There are printed, standardized tests which enable you to determine a child's deficiencies in reading skills. These tests are published by a number of companies and are available at relatively low cost. (These are not the regular standardized tests which are indicators of a child's reading level. A study of the questions a child answers incorrectly on such a test will give you some information, but not very much. The very poor reader may answer one or two questions (of over one hundred) correctly. An analysis of this test would be of very little value.)

One test that you can use we call Key Two. To compose Key Two, you will need phonics and reading workbooks. From these select a series of sheets, one for each of the 45 different sounds in our language. Figure 4-1 is an example of such a sheet. Try to find material which begins with simple exercises and goes on to the more complex exercises.

Duplicate these sheets and put them together in groups. Each group should contain from three to five sheets. Use these sheets with children who have reading problems. Have the child work on the exercises with someone who can listen as he or she reads the material. This might be you, a paraprofessional assistant, a student teacher, or even another student in the class. It might also be a parent or older sibling at home.

After the child has mastered a group, check his or her work. This checking should be done by the teacher. Of course, it isn't necessary to listen to the child read an entire page. Select samples from sections throughout each sheet.

After the pupil has completed this work, review it by having him or her read each word aloud, followed by its definition.

To reinforce this learning, hand cards may be prepared with the word on one side and the definition on the other. Then a game similar to the one outlined in Key One may be played.

Worksheets of this type may be prepared relatively easily using a school dictionary. (A more advanced dictionary gives more complex definitions, which makes the task of writing the cards more difficult.)

*How to Teach Phonics—*Key Three

Some years ago, a method called "reading by sight" came into vogue. It was adequate for bright children, who, we believe, would

Triple Consonant Blends—SCR

All of words which follow begin with the triple consonant blend SCR.

Match the word with its meaning:

1.	Scrabble	( )	a stingy man
2.	scramble	( )	a frame covered with a mesh wire
3.	Scranton	( )	to tear the surface of the skin
4.	scrap	( )	a thin, nail-like piece of metal
5.	scrape	( )	to write in badly formed letters
6.	screen	( )	to wash by hard rubbing
7.	scratch	( )	a word game
8.	screw	( )	handwriting
9.	scrawl	( )	to move along on hands and feet
10.	scrub	( )	to write hastily and carelessly
11.	script	( )	a city in Pennsylvania
12.	scribble	( )	close examination
13.	scroll	( )	to remove by rubbing with something sharp
14.	scrutiny	( )	a rolled up manuscript
15.	Scrooge	( )	a small piece

Figure 4-1

learn to read by themselves, if necessary. For others, it was a poor and often totally useless method of learning. The youngster mentioned at the beginning of this chapter, Betty Sue, was a perfect example of how the method could fail. She had no idea of how to go about deciphering a word; she had none of the skills that we call "word attack skills."

The teaching of phonics must be your next approach. It is the key to deciphering words. Let's make it Key Three. For the child with problems, Key Two will have given you the information you need, and Key Three will give you the materials with which to work.

If you possibly can, obtain a series of phonics workbooks which are on the intellectual level of your students or possibly even a bit above.

If you cannot purchase the workbooks you need, you can use sample or single copies to prepare the materials your children require. You can also write your own and can have excellent lessons while doing so. For example, you can tell your class, "We need some phonics materials to teach the combination of letters 'ea.' Let's see what words we can think of." You can work up a list of words on the board. Then say, "Now comes the fun. Who wants to give us a sentence with which we can begin?" Write several sentences on the board. Next, ask the class, "Which shall we use as our first sentence? We need to use all of the words." Work out a composition. This can then be used as part of Key Three. You'll need many pages. Save them from year to year. You'll find them extremely useful. Other word games are equally effective.

The *Be a Better Reader* series by Nila Blanton Smith, published by Prentice-Hall, contains the type of material which can be used very effectively for the teaching of the various skills many children of intermediate school age with reading problems lack. Phonics is taught in excellent units which are not insulting to the older children's intelligence.

For younger children, Harper & Row's "Design for Reading" has excellent phonics workbooks. (Gretchen Barton, Educational Consultant.)

How to Teach the Use of Configuration Clues—Key Four

Other word attack skills include configuration clues and context clues.

The appearance of a word (the combination and positioning of long and short letters), the length of the word, and the location of the letters are all factors which contribute to the configuration of a word. Some words are recognizable to a youngster by their configuration and/or because the child is able to read several of the letters. There are words, too, which are memorable because the letters describe them. "Tall" is such a word. Three of the four letters are tall. Or consider "Moon." Two of the letters are, you've guessed it, round like the moon.

You can help a child to remember some words because of

their configurations. If the child does learn to read the word, the reason he can read it is totally unimportant.

Some of the configuration clues you may want to use in your teaching are:

Double letters:
  Vowels—bee, sleep
  Consonants—hall, mirrors
Round letters—oven, cone
Tall letters—lily
Short letters—an, is
Single letter words—I, a
Two letter words—no, on
Letters below the line—jug, zip
Letters above and below the line—plant, slip

The combination of phonics with configuration clues can be of help when the configuration clue is not enough by itself. Encourage the child to use both.

Flash cards such as those described in the "hand card game" can be used effectively in connection with configuration clues. You can also use this technique to help your children to learn the words on the Dolch list.

How to Teach the Use of Context Clues—Key Five

We began this chapter with the case of Betty Sue. We had actually been relying on her ability to use context clues when we encouraged her to try to read *Jaws*. Actually she was unable to do so because of her inability to utilize phonics to help her along. When a child can use simple word attack skills, context clues can help a great deal.

Context clues are the assistance which the reading material itself offers. For example, in reading the sentence "Johnny jumped on his horse and rode away," if a child can read the words "Johnny jumped on his _____ and rode away," he or she will usually be able to "read" horse—or, really, to surmise that the word is "horse," based on the content of the material. If, however, the child has difficulty with "jumped," then he or she may not surmise "horse," unless it can be figured out by the use of phonics.

Context clues are of value, but the child should be encouraged to check his or her "guestimation." The sentence above could have been read "Johnny jumped into his car and rode away" and still have made sense. However, if the child had used phonics, "horse" could hardly have been mistaken for car.

It is well worth pointing out the fact that often if a word is followed immediately by a comma and another word, the second word will help to describe or define the first word. For example: "Christopher Columbus, an Italian, sailed under the Spanish flag," or "The old man, a miser, hid his money under his bed."

In order to use context clues, your children must have the words in their vocabulary. The word "miser," for example, could very well be unfamiliar to them. The context clue, then, would not be of help in reading it, but the definition contained in the sentence would be useful for teaching it as new vocabulary.

If you are teaching lessons in the use of context clues, first review the new vocabulary to be found in the lesson. Make sure that the child can recognize the words and define them. Then, when he encounters them in reading material, he will be able to use context clues to read them.

To prepare material which gives practice in the use of context clues, use fictional material or material in which the child will be interested. We've seen youngsters struggling to read dull paragraphs when they could have been getting the same practice from more relevant material. For example, consider the following:

> Who is your favorite comic character? Do you prefer Charlie Brown or possibly Little Orphan Annie? Dick Tracy has been around for a very long time. Another of the all-time favorites is Popeye. Recently, King Features, the publishers of Popeye, brought out a series of comic books in which Popeye helps the reader to learn about many different careers or occupations. Popeye discovers health careers, for example, and meets doctors, nurses, and ambulance drivers, and many other people in careers related to health. All of them explain their work to him. Would you like to read Popeye's career books? Perhaps he might help you to find the right career for you.

This paragraph provides many opportunities for your students to use context clues. You can experiment with it, pointing out context clues as the youngsters go along. Stress, however, the use of phonics to check themselves. The use of context clues should not encourage total guesswork. When combined with phonics, it doesn't.

How to Teach Vocabulary through the Use of Structural Parts of Words—Key Six

Children are often intimidated by long words. Children with reading problems are even more so. Yet, if the long word is composed of familiar parts and the child sees these parts, the entire complexion of the matter changes.

Begin by teaching groups of letters—which may be prefixes, roots, or suffixes, or merely groups of letters. Help the child to become comfortable with them. Then, gradually combine them.

For example, when very young children have learned the group of letters "all," they can easily be taught a whole series of words which contain "all"—"ball," "call," "fall," "small," and "squall" are only some of them.

Prefixes such as "a," "an," "in," and "re" are the beginnings of many words. It is our feeling that when a child learns to read a group of letters he gains confidence. Then phonics does the rest.

You can have your problem reader prepare lists of words he or she has learned which contain groups of letters or elements in common. We have found this to be very satisfying work which the children enjoy. Have the children put them on charts, and they can serve as excellent bulletin board displays.

Another way to teach structural parts of words is to have a contest. A small prize may be offered for the longest list of words containing the prefix "auto." (A word to the wise teacher. Check the dictionary. Don't select a group of letters which has too long a list of possibilities. The suffix "tion" is an example.) On a more sophisticated level, words ending in "ology," "ism," and "ist" can be used. Children, like most human beings, are competitive by nature. Contests, therefore, add spice to life. This is one area where they are easily developed and well received. It is unfair, however, to allow the children to work on different structural parts. It is impossible to find as many words for "tele" as for "in," for example.

How to Teach Reading Comprehension—Key Seven

The ability to recognize a word (or figure it out) is only one part of the reading process. Understanding it, and therefore comprehending what is read, is the second part of the process. Just as there are many skills involved in that first part, there are many in the second.

A.   Literal comprehension

The simplest type of comprehension we expect of the child is literal. Can he or she answer factual questions based on the material?

1.   Who or what is the material written about?
2.   Did anything happen to this person or thing?
3.   Is the material descriptive? Does it tell about someone or something?
4.   Did the material cover a particular time or place?
5.   What is the main idea of the material?

This series of questions can be helpful in teaching the comprehension of any material. Ask your youngsters to give you the answers to these questions in their own words. While this is not preparation for many standardized tests, it will help them in their thinking.

Consider the following paragraph:

In the Black Hills of South Dakota stands a monument to the greatness of America. It consists of four huge statues, each 60 feet high: George Washington, Thomas Jefferson, Abraham Lincoln, and Theodore Roosevelt. In spite of their great size (60 feet is the height of a six-story building), the men look surprisingly lifelike, and their expressions seem to change as the sunlight shines on them from different angles. The monument was the work of an inspired sculptor, Gutson Borglum, who wanted to create a memorial which would last as long as the Black Hills. His creation, once seen, can never be forgotten. It is as if these Presidents, long dead, are watching over us, reminding us of their parts in the brilliant experiment in democracy called the United States of America.

B. Interpretation

Just as the questions above call attention to the factual material in the paragraph, we can ask other questions which will help the reader interpret the material he or she is reading.

   1. Why did the author write this particular paragraph?
   2. How did the author feel about the subject?
   3. What words, phrases, or sentences tell the reader what the author's feelings were?

In the case of the paragraph above, many questions may be asked which would show whether or not the reader comprehended what he or she had read. For example:

   1. Why did Borglum choose to carve figures 60 feet high?
   2. Why did he choose the four Presidents: Washington, Jefferson, Lincoln, and Theodore Roosevelt?
   3. What can you tell about Borglum from this paragraph?

In order to comprehend what he or she has read, a child must understand word meanings. If, for example, the meaning of monument is not known, how can the rest of the paragraph be meaningful? Therefore, at the beginning of every reading lesson which introduces new material, go over the new vocabulary first. In this sample paragraph, if your children were sixth graders, you'd want to make sure they knew:

monument, greatness, huge, surprisingly, lifelike, expressions, angles, inspired, sculptor, create, memorial, creation, brilliant, experiment, democracy

They would probably know some of them, but not all. Yet, in order to comprehend the paragraph, they would need to know most of these words.

How to Prepare Reading Activities

You can use newspaper or magazine articles to construct reading activities your children will enjoy. Paste the article on an oaktag card along with one or more of the activities listed below.

Instruct the children to do any writing or drawing necessary on a separate sheet of paper.

Here are some possible activities:
1. Tell what you would do if you were in this position (or if this happened to you).
2. Pick out the main idea of this article. Why did the person write it?
3. Give this article a headline.
4. Pick out three words you didn't know before. Write them in your notebook; then look up the definition for each and write it next to the word.
5. Pick out three words which have the phonic element (   ) in them. (Insert an element.)
6. Pick out the main idea and then three sentences which support or explain the main idea.
7. Pick out the words in this article which rhyme with: (give rhyming words).
8. Select five nouns from this article which rhyme with: (give rhyming words).
9. Select five verbs (or adjectives or adverbs) and use each in a new sentence.
10. Write five questions about this article.
11. Select five words from this article describing people (or places or actions).
12. Select three words or phrases which told you how the person in this article felt (or how the person who wrote it felt).
13. Fill in the words which answer the questions below. (Use factual questions.)
14. List examples from this paragraph to show: (any trait might be listed here).

By using relatively short articles which are of high interest, you do not intimidate the child with a reading problem. Often he or she is frightened off by long stories and by small print.

How to Teach Children to Read for Detail—Key Eight

As adults, we know how important the small print on a label or in a contract can be. This small print may contain important details. As our pupils learn to read, they should be taught to read for detail and to be impressed by certain details. One excellent learning experience you can give them is to have them read as many labels on products they have in their homes as is necessary until they find one which is dangerous to their health. (You may or may not want to exclude cigarettes because as soon as you use the phrase "dangerous to your health," they'll probably recognize it and associate it with the Surgeon General's warning.) Don't give any more clues than that. Ask that they bring in the article or copy the warning. Have the pupils read each label in class and discuss each one carefully. Pay particular attention to poisons and antidotes and take the time to explain each fully. This might be considered digressing from the teaching of reading, but it might also someday save a person's life. This type of reading for detail should definitely be taught in class as a most important lesson.

You should also teach the skill of selecting details which help the reader to understand the main ideas of paragraphs.

Stunt Men

When a movie is being filmed, stunt men are used in dangerous situations. Have you ever seen a car chase or a violent collision in a movie? The driver of that car wasn't the movie star you thought he was—or whom you saw sitting in the driver's seat. It was a stunt man who took his place as soon as the close up was over. Movie stars rarely do their own bronco-busting or fighting, either. Even the great Tarzan didn't swing from tree to tree. A stunt man is a professional who earns his livelihood taking risks for someone else. This can be a very dangerous business.

The details given in this paragraph, which show how dangerous the work of the stunt man is, can easily be selected by the pupil reading it.

Being able to select details is very important in every other school subject. In science and social studies, facts or details are needed for their own sake and also as a basis for making generalizations. In mathematics, without the details, problem-solving is impossible. Therefore, as you teach every subject and instruct your students to read for details, you're also teaching them reading skills. Remember that if students do poorly in math, it may be because they lack the ability to read for details.

How to Teach the Use of the Dictionary—Key Nine

The dictionary can be of great help in the teaching of reading. However, the edition used must be suitable to the children's intellectual capability. The *Winston Dictionary for Schools* (published by Holt, Rinehart and Winston, Inc.) is excellent for the intermediate grades. Figure 4-2 lists the uses of the dictionary.

Uses of the Dictionary

1. The main listing gives the spelling and syllabification.
2. This is followed by the pronunciation and the syllable accented.
3. Next comes the part of speech the word is.
4. Then the plural (if the word is a noun) or special parts (of verbs) are listed.
5. If the word is an adjective, the comparative and suprelative forms are given.
6. Irregular forms of adverbs are included.
7. The definition or definitions of each word follow.

Figure 4-2

As soon as your pupils have learned phonics, you can teach them the symbols used to indicate pronunciation.

Instilling the habit of using the dictionary whenever a question arises regarding a word's meanings or when a *possible* spelling is known is eminently worthwhile.

We have encouraged youngsters to browse through their dictionaries when they have a few minutes to spare. They report having enjoyed the experience. One day, we heard a young man exclaim, "That's how you spell 'abacus.' I always thought it had a 'K.' " He'd learned something—and been pleased by it.

Parents Guide

Parents should be encouraged to help their children improve their reading. Figure 4-3 is an example of material that can be distributed to parents for this purpose.

Note: To All Parents.

Suggestions to Help Your Child Improve in Reading

1. *Patience*—this is a long haul.
2. *Acceptance*—Never scold, never reproach. Remember that you are there to help your son or daughter improve in reading.
3. *Flexibility*—Each subject may be taught in many ways; try to devise different ways yourself.
4. *Praise*—as much as you can when genuine success is evident.

Tips on Techniques

1. Have your child keep a hard cover notebook or a set of index cards with the new words learned (together with their definitions).
2. Find a book which is interesting to your child and is slightly above his reading level. Use the public library as much as possible.
3. Tabloid newspapers, comic books, and picture magazines frequently appeal to children. Use these materials at the appropriate reading level to teach critical evaluation of reading material.

Figure 4-3

4. Trips to museums, places of historic interest, and so on are valuable as a motivating device for reading. Encourage your child to read captions, labels, posters, and signs.
5. Make a great effort to associate reading with pleasure and always encourage self-expression.
6. Always relate reading to vocational goals and/or concrete practical experiences that occur in your child's life.
7. Common Sight Words. Some words are encountered so frequently in reading that it is helpful to learn them very quickly. Make sure that your child is familiar with *all* the words below.

about	best	cut	for	help	know
after	better	did	found	her	let
again	big	do	four	here	light
all	black	does	from	him	like
always	blue	done	full	his	little
am	both	don't	funny	hold	live
an	boy	down	gave	hot	long
and	bring	draw	get	how	look
any	brown	drink	give	hurt	made
are	but	eat	go	I	make
around	buy	eight	going	if	many
as	by	every	goes	in	may
ask	call	exit	good	into	me
at	came	fall	got	is	men
ate	can	far	green	it	much
away	carry	fast	grow	its	must
be	clean	find	had	jump	my
because	cold	first	has	just	myself
been	come	five	have	keep	never
before	could	fly	he	kind	new

Figure 4-3 (cont'd.)

no	play	she	the	under	when
not	please	show	their	up	where
now	pretty	sing	them	upon	which
of	pull	sit	then	us	white
off	put	six	there	use	who
old	ran	sleep	these	very	why
on	read	small	they	walk	will
once	ride	so	think	want	wish
one	right	some	this	warm	with
only	round	soon	those	was	work
open	run	start	three	wash	would
or	said	stop	to	we	write
our	saw	take	today	well	yellow
out	say	tell	too	went	yes
over	see	ten	try	were	you
own	seven	thank	two	what	your
pick	shall	that			

Developing Comprehension Skills

1. Comprehension, as well as vocabulary, is sharpened through the use of oral discussion:
   • Discussions centering on current matters of interest
   • Discussions relating to mass media (radio, TV)
   • Discussions relating to visits
2. Making lists of words in interesting categories will increase vocabulary. For example: Compile a list of words for preparing a meal (food, sugar, meat, stove, oven), for repairing automobiles (car, engine, carburetor, mile), and so on.
3. Selecting the main idea:
   • Make up a title for a story discussion or TV or radio program.

Figure 4-3 (cont'd.)

- Tell or write a summary of the story or discussion.
- Select the most important sentence.

4. Organization of ideas
   - Tell what happened in chronological order.
   - Find the answers to the questions who, what, when, where, why, and how.

5. Find details
   - Find the answers to specific questions.

6. Drawing inferences
   - Complete a story
   - Anticipate what will happen next in a story or in current events.
   - Draw conclusions from information given.
   - Interpret the meaning of a sentence or paragraph.

7. Study Skills
   - Alaphabet using
   - Locating information through the use of:
     Title page
     Table of contents
     Maps, diagrams
     Glossary, index
     Dictionary
     Encyclopedia
     Graphs
     Bibliography
   - Organizing information
     Listing
     Classifying
     Skimming
     Summarizing
     Note-taking
     Rereading to aid retention

8. Sounding out Unfamiliar Words
   - Consonant
   - Short Vowels
   - Long Vowels

Figure 4-3 (cont'd.)

- Consonant Combination
  (play, clock, flame, glass, blow; also SH—shop, CH—chin, TH—thing, WH—whiff)
- Additional Vowel Sounds
  oo as in soon
  oo as in book
  oi as in oil
  ow as in owl
  ar as in bar
  ir as in fir
  ur as in burn
  ow as in slow
  au as in maul
  ay as in day
  y as in my

9. Analyzing Parts of Words
   - Compound word
     newspaper—news paper
     cannot—can not
   - Base or root word and common word endings:
     asked
     rained
     asking
     raining
     asks
     rainy
   - Prefixes:
     re
     fill
     tell
     dis
     like
     appear
     un
     even
     true

Figure 4-3 (cont'd.)

- Suffixes:
    ly
    er
    est
    tion
    ness
    ful
    any
    ous
    ious
    ent
    ful—wonderful
        careful
    ly—quickly
        sweetly
- Divide words into *syllables*

We are sure that the material above will be of help to you as you work with your youngster to improve his or her reading.

Figure 4-3 (cont'd.)

Chapter 5

How to Deal with Children
Who Have Problems Learning Arithmetic

Dr. Mitchell Lazarus,[1] writing in the Education section of the *Saturday Review,* states in his article "Rx for Mathophobia," "Mathematics—that great inspirer of fear and loathing—would not be a bugaboo if it were geared more closely to everyday reality and presented in less arid and abstract terms." He quotes Jerrold Zacharias, noted physicist and educator of MIT, who calls the problem "mathophobia, a fear of mathematics." Why should this be true? Why should there be many adults who remember their math classes with distaste? Why should there be children suffering day by day? In this chapter, we shall show you how to change that—how to make mathematics actually pleasant for your students and, incidentally, for yourself.

As you know, human beings develop at different rates; this includes intellectual as well as physical development. However, while educators would all agree with this concept, when it comes to applying it in their classrooms they sometimes forget it. For example, even as early as the first grade there are differences. Some children will learn everything you teach them with seemingly little

---

[1]Lazarus, Mitchell. "RX for Mathophobia," *Saturday Review,* June 28, 1975, Saturday Review/World, Inc., 488 Madison Avenue, New York City, New York 10022

effort. Others will not. This fact may be evident, or it may be hidden from view. In the case of arithmetic, children who are having difficulties are usually noticeable. They're the little ones who don't do well on tests. They can add three plus four but then run into trouble with three plus eight. As a general rule, they go on to the next grade in spite of the fact that they haven't mastered even the simplest of mathematical facts. Then, in the second grade, as new work is presented, they become more and more befuddled. Their attempts at doing even simple examples are often pitifully futile. *But they usually are pushed ahead.* Our concentration has been for the most part on why children can't read. Never mind that they can't do arithmetic.

It is our belief that no child can handle arithmetic if his foundation is poor and that no matter what grade he is in, without the ability to add, subtract, multiply, divide, and handle fractions and decimals, he is lost, mathematically speaking.

We have seen a great deal of time spent on abstract mathematics. We read of young children being taught algebra, and we wonder if there is some reason that educators are so blind. We've been sold bills of goods about careers in the future. (For example, we are told that in 1980 a large percentage of our population will be doing jobs which do not exist today. Even if this is so, who says they will involve algebra?) As our reader has already discovered, we are entirely in favor of children being given as much material as they can master, enriching their programs as much as possible, but *not at the expense of the fundamentals. We have to go back to the fundamentals.* We feel we are truly in the avant-garde of education in saying this because eventually educators are going to come to this realization—and we invite you to join us. Furthermore, your children will benefit tremendously.

This chapter has been written to help you to institute a program which will really help children with problems learning mathematics.

Why Study Arithmetic and Mathematics?

More than in any other subject, the benefits of knowing arithmetic and mathematics have been obscured. One of the things we will be doing throughout this chapter is showing how to use everyday situations to teach mathematics. We will suggest that you constantly use devices, examples, and techniques which show how valuable a knowledge of mathematics can be and exactly how important it is in everyday life. Devote several lessons to the topic, "Why I need to learn arithmetic (or mathematics)." Make these very personal. In one of these lessons, divide the class up into buzz groups of five or six students each. Have the groups list as many reasons as they can. Each group should have a secretary to record these. After twenty minutes reconvene the class and have the reasons listed on the board. Go around the room, asking each group for one reason. After each group has contributed, go around a second time and hopefully even a third time. (Tell the groups that they are to consider the reasons for knowing mathematics now as well as in the future.)

One time the reason a child gave for learning mathematics was, "I want to get married, and I'll have to be able to handle money." The next child to be asked responded, "I have to handle money right now. I get an allowance." Have the children think of as many reasons as they can. Many will respond with far more mature answers than you'd expect—"I'll have to pay taxes," for instance.

Practicality is one aspect of arithmetic and mathematics teaching which has not been utilized to the fullest. Who cares if a train is going sixty miles an hour in a western direction and the wind is blowing thirty miles an hour north? Which way is the smoke going? Who cares—and why should they? But if gasoline prices go up from 68 cents per gallon to 90 cents per gallon the children care. There is a point to teaching it.

The next lesson should be devoted to zeroing in on the individual. "What dealings do you have which require you to use arithmetic or mathematics skills?" you ask. Have each child think about his entire day, week, and month. Point out the little things— lunch money, for instance.

To further use everyday examples, we suggest that you adopt a people-to-people approach. Have guests come in to speak to your students about how important arithmetic and mathematics skills are to them. For instance, if there is a member of your class whose parent is involved in consumerism (a subscriber to *Consumer Reports* might be one such individual), perhaps he or she would speak to the class regarding this important topic. A discussion on how to shop wisely could convince the children of the need for a knowledge of arithmetic on an everyday basis.

A discussion on checking accounts could also show the use of arithmetic by everyone. A representative of a local business bank would be able to show how important it is to be able to work with numbers correctly. A carpenter, a pharmacist, an engineer, a nurse, a merchant—any of these people would be able to bring home the need for arithmetic and mathematics skills. Children are far more willing to learn something if they see the need for it, and being shown the need by a person other than the teacher carries a lot of weight with it. Check with your class—you'll often find parents engaged in occupations which involve arithmetic or mathematics and which show the value of this knowledge to every person.

This type of motivation is used to create an intrinsic need in the children. These intrinsic needs are excellent because they foster a real, not an artificial, desire. It is not: "I have to learn this because I want to pass the test."

How to Use Diagnosis to Spot Difficulties

You must know what you are doing when you teach skills. Just as you must know where a child is lacking specific skills in reading, you need to know what skills he or she is lacking in arithmetic.

Assemble a test which you can use for diagnostic purposes. You can easily use the questions at the end of each chapter in textbooks (sometimes they are located at the end of the textbook). Prepare to spend time developing this test, because you will probably use it year after year. Begin with simple addition and proceed through every topic your children have already been taught. The length of the test will depend on the grade the children are in. Give from eight to ten examples per topic so that you can spot inadequacies.

Diagnostic Test—Mathematics

A. Circle the closest estimate. (Be prepared to explain how you arrived at that estimate.)

1. $28 + 29 + 21 + 6 =$ 50   65   90   100
2. $7 + 46 + 32 + 24 =$ 70   130   80   110
3. $82 - 39 =$ 70   40   90   50
4. $192 - 69 =$ 120   90   110   150

B. Write estimate (to the nearest hundred) only:

     $456 + 861 + 326$
     $169 + 864 + 689$
      $45 + 356 + 957$
  $1,233 + 456 + 789$
     $269 - 140$
  $2,310 - 832$

C. Add:

16	17013
28	7013
44	701
3	70

D. Add:
1) $132 + \ \ 27 + 276$
2) $634 + 276 + \ \ 40$

E. Find the total: 42, 133, 31, 17, 6
F. Find the sum: 3,456; 7,890; 22
G. From $78 take $6.95.
H. Subtract 292 from 1,000.
I.   1.   Take 2,339 from 7,893.
     2.   Take $3.98 from $20.00.
     3.   Take $24.95 from $100.00.
J. $1,678 - 99$
K. Find the remainder:

8,765	808	789
- 4,398	- 399	- 98

L. Find the missing number:

8,763	537
-	-
4,521	268

Figure 5-1

A suggested pre-test for the addition and subtraction of whole numbers (for seventh grade students) might look like Figure 5-1.

Explain to your children exactly what you are doing. You have already discussed why they need to learn arithmetic, now you are showing them what skills they need to know and where they are deficient in these skills.

Recently, the principal of an intermediate school asked a group of bright children to solve a problem for him. He gave them the following information: "I went to the supermarket," he said. "I bought these items: one dozen eggs at 79¢, one loaf of bread at 45¢, three cans of tomato sauce at the rate of 2 for 59¢, a pound of meat at $1.89, and three containers of milk at 39¢ each. How much did I spend?" *This was a bright class.* One-third of the children did not solve this problem correctly. They were not able to list the prices or figure out the cost of the three cans of tomato sauce. Some made errors in the addition. This is, unfortunately, not in the least unusual. We've lost sight of the fundamentals.

When you design your test, use the textbooks of previous grades to give you the materials you need. After addition, subtraction, multiplication, division, fractions, decimals, and measurement, include sample problems. They need not be tricky. In fact, there is no point to their being tricky.

This is your chance to educate yourself. You will find this test to be absolutely essential. Furthermore, you can use it as a pre-test and then, with the current year's work added, as a post-test.

"We've had this test before," your children will tell you.

"Right. Let's see exactly how much you've learned," you would answer. Then add the comment, "I would be delighted, absolutely thrilled, if every one of you gets 100%." Unfortunately, they won't, but they'll improve if you use the test well.

How to Teach Fundamentals

Those children who have problems with arithmetic or mathematics almost always cannot handle the fundamentals. It is disconcerting for a teacher to discover children who cannot accurately count to ten in the third grade, but this has actually happened—and more than once.

If you feel that it is necessary, then privately have those children who are very slow count for you. And don't be too shocked. If they need to learn to count, that is your starting point.

Teach the vocabulary:

It seems to us that with the passage of time the use of the English language has fallen lower and lower. A trip to the movies bears this out. Then, too, there are youngsters whose parents never talk to them. The parents will point, for instance, to an object. "Get me that," they say. And the child does not learn what the name of "that" is. Many children come from homes where parents don't want to be bothered. These children have been conditioned to never ask questions. If such a child is in your class, he or she may never ask you what "equal" means—and never know. Therefore, for every word you use check to be sure that each child knows its meaning. If the children feel that you honestly want them to know, they become less ashamed of asking. Keep repeating, "If I use a word you don't know or understand, please raise your hand." By saying this over and over you reduce their anxiety or you may break through their pattern of parentally induced indifference.

Once you've reviewed your diagnostic tests, take action.

Give every child, whether he or she has a problem learning arithmetic or not, credit for having intelligence. Place the responsibility on his or her shoulders. Say kindly, "I can see by your pretest that you haven't learned your multiplication facts. You know them for two, three, and four, but not for five, six, seven, eight, and nine. I have a plan for you. I know that you can learn them. Will you take the responsibility for trying to learn this material?" You may use the "mature" aspect here, too, if you wish. Once the child has agreed, work out a plan with him or her.

The first thing you have to do is teach him or her the material. Sometimes it has never been taught thoroughly before. Sometimes it's been taught, but the child did not receive it. Many times material is not "received" because the child was not ready for it. Just as there is "reading readiness" so is there "arithmetical readiness." At any rate, and for whatever reason, when a child cannot handle the fundamentals, you must teach him.

Begin with real materials whenever possible. We saw one teacher use packages of buttons. They proved an excellent tool in teaching addition, subtraction, and multiplication. An abacus can be used, or a similar object can be created with strings of beads. In whatever way you prefer, use materials that allow the youngsters to manipulate objects to see that if there are four rows of objects and each row has five objects, there is a total of twenty objects. A very creative teacher used a pumpkin to teach division. She roasted it, and the children actually cut it up. They divided the seeds among the class, too, and made montages with the seeds, rice, and macaroni. A box of macaroni or ziti can provide manipulative objects, too.

Whenever you can, teach the child who has a problem by using real objects first. Only after the youngster has received what you are teaching should you proceed to any sort of abstraction.

As with the teaching of children who have reading problems, there is no reason for you to do all this teaching yourself. However, you should train the people you expect to teach— paraprofessionals, parents, siblings, or classmates. Be sure that they know exactly what you want taught and how you want it presented. We cannot emphasize strongly enough exactly how important this training is. Remember mathophobia. Many parents suffer from it and feel insecure so that they are literally afraid to attempt any teaching or tutoring of math. To counteract this problem, make your instructions as clear as possible. Put them in writing at the top of each work or assignment sheet you give out. Be sure that the children understand them fully, too, so that if there is a question they may be able to answer it.

When you give a child an assignment or worksheet, stress the concept that it is his or her responsibility to complete the assignment. Don't allow him or her to come away with the notion that it's anyone else's. Training in the acceptance of responsibility is as important as training in arithmetic.

Flash cards are a very successful device for teaching mathematics, too. Workbooks and exercise sections of the textbook are also good.

How to Reinforce Learning and Make Reinforcement Fun

Select a small portion of the work to be learned. Don't ask the youngster to learn several facts in one fell swoop. Work on a few until the youngster has mastered those. When he or she has mastered these facts, give him or her some token of recognition. One elementary school teacher very successfully used a chart headed, "We Took a Giant Step Today." It was a very large chart, and every time a child achieved a goal, he or she was given a cut-out of a foot on which he or she wrote his or her name and the date. This "foot" was then stapled on the chart. There was no indication of what goal had been achieved, so no one could possibly be embarrassed. No goal was too big or too small to be recorded.

Are you wondering if you can spend time teaching a seventh grader to multiply by six? Not only can you, you have to if he or she is unable to do so. How does the teacher learn this? How do you learn which skills are missing? By diagnosing from the test you've given.

You may find it effective when you discover that a child has difficulty dividing to make another diagnosis using a new set of examples. Begin this set with the most basic of fundamentals and progress to the point at which a child in that grade should be. Explain to the girls and boys that this is for diagnostic purposes. They generally respond very favorably to this type of teaching.

Be absolutely, painfully honest. We heard one child say, "No one ever told me before that I had to understand decimals. So I never paid attention." Until that time, he never did!

In going over the fundamentals, try to make the teaching as much of a game and as little of a bore as you possibly can. For instance, you have children who have trouble adding. Buy one of the new dart boards that use magnetized darts rather than darts with pointed ends. Create as many games as you can think of. In *Successful Methods for Teaching the Slow Learner*,[2] we have outlined a number of them. The game which follows is fun, simple, and teaches addition and subtraction.

---

[2]Karlin, M.S. and Berger, R. *Successful Methods for Teaching the Slow Learner*, Parker Publishing Co. Inc., West Nyack, N.Y., 1969.

The Weight Game

Bring in a scale. Weigh each child and tell him or her the weight. Then use the weights. For instance, how much weight is on the floor of this room? If ten students (specify which ten) were to get into an elevator, how much would they weigh? (This can be made more exciting if you actually visit a place with an elevator and check the allowable weights.) With the current interest in calories, you can have older children do all sorts of addition involving them. *When a child realizes that he or she is having difficulty pursuing these activities, give simple work drilling the particular skill needed.* (If you are using weight as the basis for any activity, be sure that no child is upset because he or she is sensitive about being over- or under-weight.)

Another interesting project which can utilize skills is checking the weather reports. Have the children note the temperature at the same time each day for one month. (As an added fillip, you can have them check the weather against the forecast. Have them note the forecast from a particular news program each evening. It becomes too complex to use advance forecasts, although that's fun, too. But using one day at a time is easier.) Have the pupil write down the forecast and the temperature for the day. Then, after one month, you have many statistics with which to work. For example, the temperatures can be averaged.

From taking the daily temperature readings, you can go on to checking an almanac. This can be great fun, because almanacs are really forecasts made months or years in advance. Your students can be adding or subtracting without realizing that these are practice drills.

For those children who love sports, batting averages, pennant races, and all sorts of sports records can be utilized to give the pupils experience in dealing with fundamentals.

Problems dealing with the pupils' money can best be prepared by the youngsters themselves. Tell them that they are going to work on a budget for a person their age. Use an imaginary child. Ask students how much allowance this child gets. Then have the pupils give you amounts of money to be spent. (Many pupils have absolutely no concept of budgeting. This is an important concept.) You may want to have the child earn some money from a paper route to give you more capital with which to work.

It's most important that you discuss the spending of money. It is surprising how many pupils can't "make change." The child with a problem in arithmetic most often falls into this category. Not too long ago a pharmacist friend was looking for a young man to work as a clerk in one of his stores. He put a sign in the window, and almost immediately a young man appeared. Well dressed and polite, he asked if he could work in the back of the store. Upon questioning, it turned out that he could not change a dollar bill correctly. Not even a dollar bill! He was not mentally retarded, but he had developed a mental block in regard to arithmetic! He told the pharmacist that he had had trouble with a teacher, so he never went to school!

Hands-On Experiences

As the interest in career education increases, more and more teachers are giving their children hands-on experiences. In the case of children with problems in arithmetic skills, these can be highly effective. One of the most easily accomplished of these experiences is the operation of a store. There are a number of ways in which this store may be established.

What will we sell? The products tht you will be selling will probably be determined by the age of your students, the policies of the administration, and the time you decide to spend on the project. You'll find, however, that this is a good project and that you can teach many relevant lessons to the children, including costs, profits, and even losses, through this activity.

What are some possible products? You could sell school supplies—pencils, pens, crayons, notebooks, book covers, notebook paper, erasers, and so on. You could operate a book store or even a comic-book store. You could sell used toys. You could also sell food stuffs—from candies to homemade cookies and cakes. There are many possibilities.

The choice of the items you will sell in the store should be made by the students and possibly by the parents. If the teacher makes the decision, it may turn out to be a dud.

When children purchase new merchandise there is no need for a "chit" system, but with most of the items we've listed above the use of credits or chits is very worthwhile. If a child brings in an item, he receives credit for it, which he can then spend for other items. In this way an artificial monetary system is established.

Many schools have run stores on a school-wide basis, and you can work with other teachers if you prefer. However, to give your students as much experience working with money as possible, it is advisable to keep the store within your class, although you can certainly sell to other classes. (Permission is needed from the administration for this, of course. However, it is definitely an arithmetic or mathematics project—with career education overtones.)

Building the Store

You can have your children decide where they want to put the store and then measure the floor space to see how large the shelves and other equipment they plan to use can be. They can build a shop from cartons, which can be cardboard or wood, depending on what is available. Remember that you will be dealing in three dimensions, which will give the children real experience in the area of spatial concepts. If you decide to have small bins constructed, children will get more experience in measuring and planning. (Try to structure activities which require measuring and planning. Don't use a series of shoe boxes unless you do not need to include the experiences of measuring and planning.)

Have the children make signs. What the signs say will depend on the merchandise they will be selling and the market they will be selling to. If the market is to be the entire school, extensive sign making will be necessary. For instance, every sign must be within certain size limitations, and the letters must be of specific sizes, too.

Don't rush this project, but don't allow it to drag along, either. You can get interest to a high pitch by working at it rapidly.

Assign specific jobs to each of the students. They may sell, prepare stock, make change (cashiering), and so on. Allow different children to act as managers and actually manage the store. Give the girls and boys as much responsibility as you can. You may have to have a squad of "shoppers" as they do in department stores to be sure that merchandise is not stolen. (This is, in fact, an excellent idea, because shoplifting has become a very serious problem among teenagers.)

If you use chits, have the children make them out of special paper. You have to be sure that no one can duplicate the chits and distribute them gratis to their friends. Use the denominations we have in our currency—pennies, nickels, dimes, quarters, half-dollars, and dollars.

We recall one young lady who "felt like a millionaire" because she had brought in a pair of ice skates and had gotten so many chits for them that she had fun finding other items she wanted to buy.

Make sure that the child who has arithmetic problems works on them so that he or she can participate and really enjoy this project.

School-Wide Candy Sales

One of the fund raisers we have used very successfully is the school-wide candy sale. We have found that it has bolstered the egos of many children who are non-academically oriented. If you get the teachers in the math department to explain the bookkeeping procedures carefully and you review the method to use to give a customer change, the children will learn mathematics as well as fund-raising. Since the plan we use includes "prizes" for the youngsters even if they only sell one box of candy, most of the children participate.

We have found that we can increase the excitement by announcing on the public address system the total number of sales so far and then asking the youngsters to estimate the number sold that day. Mathematics teachers have helped them with the calculations, and often there are "guesstimations" which come very close.

The children are told exactly how much money they earn and the uses to which the money is to be put. In this way, they can see that they are all working for the benefit of the school as a whole and, in addition, earning prizes for themselves. Candy sales have proven useful for raising morale, giving practice in the handling of money, and helping children see the results of labor. Since any child who does not wish to do so does not participate, and since no mention is ever made of this, no one is made uncomfortable.

How to Motivate Older Students
to Learn Arithmetic

Many of the older students who are not at all interested in school will change completely, as far as arithmetic is concerned, if the topic you choose for them is related to automobiles, motorcycles, or stereos.

"Let's talk about cars," you might begin. Suddenly there are eyes looking at you who haven't bothered for days. "What's your favorite car?" That will usually bring a response from even the most alienated student. If this doesn't work, bring him into the conversation by asking the question of him and then inquiring, "Why do you like it?"

This discussion should take a period or so. Before the end of the discussion ask if students can bring in some owner's manuals from any cars so that the class can compare them. Be equipped with several of your own. (Car dealers or manufacturers can help you with this. Write to the latter if you can't obtain any from the former.)

Now you can ask the students to compare the various specifications—anything from the size of the car to the amount of gasoline used. Prepare questions which require calculations in advance. Ask the students to prepare others. This is the type of assignment that they can really become involved in. Another interesting project can be carried out if you have obtained manuals from older cars and can compare them with newer ones.

From this, the discussion and problems can move into costs. What are the costs of buying, operating, and maintaining a car? What are the differences between the more expensive cars and the less expensive ones? What about insurance? With all of this material, you are supplying relevant information and preparing the youngsters for the near future—when they will be driving cars. You can even bring in safety measures, including the length of time it takes for a car to come to a stop after the brakes have been applied, according to the speed at which the car was traveling.

You will find that some girls will not become as involved in this project as boys, but it is worth pursuing it nevertheless. Stereos, record players, and records offer another area to interest "turned off" students. Costs and comparisons make for interesting, relevant information.

How to Motivate Children to Learn Number Facts through Mock Checking Accounts

The use of whole numbers and decimals can be taught at the same time that you are teaching another very important skill needed for everyday living. We're talking about keeping a checkbook. This skill, which is really relatively simple, has been a bone-in-the-throat for a great many people. Yet, if this skill is taught while people are young, much difficulty may be avoided later on.

Begin by making artificial checks. (Don't even be tempted to use real ones. The strangest things can happen—and why even take a chance on causing problems?) Design the checks so that they are attractive and duplicate them. You can have the children assemble checkbooks and staple them together. Now plan the check receipt book. This may be part of the checkbook or separate from it. Next, give your children each a checkbook and tell them that they have $1,000 in it. Tell them that they will have to write checks and keep track of their balances.

As was previously suggested, you may wish to have a speaker from a local bank come in to discuss how a checkbook should be kept.

Have the class suggest various expenditures. Then have them write checks for these expenditures. You may have them work independently, in small groups, or as a class. After each expenditure, have them deduct from the balance. After they have written and deducted ten checks, have them prepare a bank statement. Show them samples first and teach them what each item indicates.

Prepare a number of different lists of expenditures, duplicate

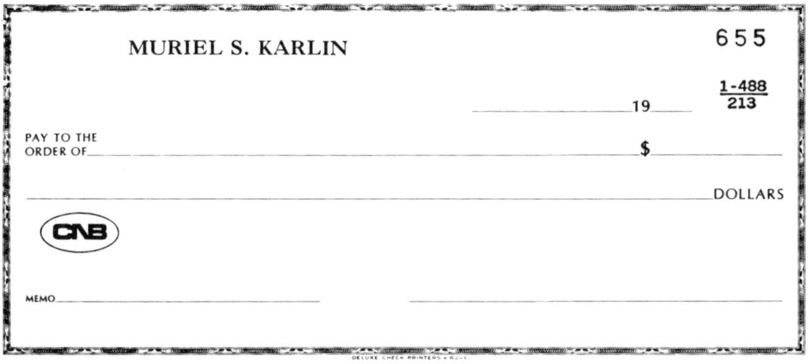
MURIEL S. KARLIN 655

1-488
213

19

PAY TO THE
ORDER OF $

DOLLARS

CNB

MEMO

Figure 5-2

these, and distribute them to the pupils so that they will be writing different checks, have different balances, and have different statements.

There is a great deal of addition and subtraction involved in these exercises. In addition to using addition and subtraction, the children are becoming familiar with the checkbook and how to handle it.

How to Use a Variety of Approaches

There are many approaches which can be used to make arithmetic and mathematics more relevant to the children's lives. You can teach students how to figure discounts. Try discussing discounts on records. You can explain taxes—especially the withholding system. You can compute the costs of smoking. (You may wish to include the costs in terms of health, too.) You can discuss the costs of traveling. For example, you can compare the cost of staying in motels with the cost of camping. You can also discuss gas mileage, tolls, and car repairs. You can teach budgeting—for young people and for families. You can use astronomy. For example, you can discuss distances between planets, the time involved in space travel, and so on. You can even use checkers and chess to teach logical thinking.

Preparing Your Own Material

Far too much of the material available in textbooks and workbooks is not relevant to the lives of the youngsters you are teaching. With this in mind, prepare your own material with the idea that what you work up can be used for many years without going out of date. Of course, you may wish to change figures occasionally, but even this will not be necessary too often.

Have your children suggest problems. Not once, but many times, teachers have used tests prepared almost entirely from the questions submitted by their pupils.

When you are using a text which is not relevant, try to show your students why you are asking them to learn the particular material. Making material seem relevant is your particular challenge. If you are teaching decimals, the relevance lies in the fact that our monetary system is based on the decimal system. We constantly use parts of things and thereby require a knowledge of how to handle fractions.

Some concepts, such as the metric system, will be needed in the near future. This can be considered a valid reason for teaching a subject. However, teachers will be hard pressed to explain the need for doing problems such as: "A grasshopper is 30 feet away from a fence. With every jump he hops half the remaining distance to the fence. How many jumps will he have to make to reach the fence?" If the students understand that a problem helps them think in a mathematical way, that's fine. If not, the problem should be changed. There is so much important material our children need to know that this type of information seems unnecessary.

Chapter 6

How to Develop Language Arts Skills

In the educational world in which we live, reading is stressed over and over again. There is no one who would deny its tremendous importance. However, there are other skills which are almost, if not as, important, and with which our pupils may have severe problems. Listening and speaking are two of these problems. Every person has the need to be able to communicate, and if a person is unable to do so, he or she will have serious difficulties. If you get a child in your class who is unable to communicate, your work to solve this problem can truly change his or her life.

How to Work on Listening Skills

Our world is just as filled with noise pollution as it is with air pollution. One of the problems some children face is the inability to sort out sounds. To train your students to ignore noise pollution and *really listen* for the purpose of learning, begin by reading a paragraph containing a number of facts to them. Then ask them to list eight things they heard you read. The paragraph might be one such as the following:

Cape Cod

Resembling a giant arm flexing its muscles, Cape Cod cuts into the sea. The Atlantic Ocean washes its eastern shores. On the south is Nantucket Sound, in which an island called Martha's Vineyard and Nantucket Island are located. Cape Cod Bay lies to the north.

Cape Cod is the pride of the state of Massachusetts. The Cape is many things to many people. It's a place for every kind of water sport from swimming to sailing and fishing. Antique hunters love it. But what makes Cape Cod unique is that it is the place where the Pilgrims landed in the year 1620. The *Mayflower,* their ship, has been remembered, as they have, ever since that November day.

After you have read the selection, divide the chalkboard in half. Ask the class to list the various items they remember. Write them on one half of the chalkboard. Next, tell the class that you will read another paragraph and repeat the experiment.

Read a similar selection, such as the following:

Crater Lake

On the top of the Cascade Mountain Range in the state of Oregon, there is an ancient volcano. This volcano is most unusual because when it erupted only the top of the volcano disintegrated. The sides remained, with a huge hole, or crater, in the center. This crater filled with rain water and formed a lake which today we call Crater Lake. It is outstanding because of its exceptionally deep blue color. Crater Lake is 6 miles across and exceptionally deep. It has a 20-mile shoreline encircled by lava cliffs 500 to 2,000 feet above sea level.

The Phantom Ship, a mass of lava rising about 160 feet above the waters of the lake, resembles a ship in full sail.

Again, ask the class to tell you as many facts as they can about the second selection.

If your experiment is successful, more items should be listed from the second selection than from the first. (Each of the selections above has approximately the same number of facts.)

Next, discuss with the pupils the reasons why they were more successful in recalling facts from the second selection than from the first (if they were). Discuss the difference between *active* and *passive* listening. If they were more successful in the first instance, it may be because the material was more relevant to their lives or more familiar to them.

One of the skills associated with listening is note taking. This skill can be taught to children as early as the fifth and sixth grades. However, you have to take into consideration the fact that note taking is a difficult and separate skill. If you expect your pupils to learn subject matter, either check the notes they take or actually give them notes from which to study.

Speaking and Listening

When you give an assignment to do a report, plan to have each child read his or her work aloud. This can serve to develop both listening and speaking skills. It can also help to develop background.

It seems to this author that our children should have heard of Caesar, Hamlet, and, of course, Shakespeare. You can introduce literature, art, music, all the humanities, while you teach listening and speaking skills. All of this can be done through reports.

Although purists may object to the use of simplified versions of Shakespeare, Charles and Mary Lamb's *Tales from Shakespeare* serves as an excellent introduction. The adventure and color is all there. Have your children read the plays and report on each one. You'll find that the class will listen. If you use the technique of questioning for details, the listening training will be highly effective.

The same method of teaching may be used for introducing any area of study. Having the children do their own research and share it with the class is far more worthwhile than having children write reports which only you and they will read.

Listening and Responding

Many children get relatively little opportunity to listen, think, and then respond orally. An excellent means to teach this skill is through debate.

One of the faults we've found with classroom debates is that they are often dominated by the same pupils who usually speak in class. It requires a highly skilled teacher to prevent this from happening. These "talkers" often need training in listening rather than in speaking.

When you are setting up a debate, decide what your goals are. A spirited discussion is one possibility. It is also possible to structure debates so that some of your pupils speak and others listen. Have the pupils who are to *listen judge* the debate, while the ones you want to receive training in speaking actually participate in it.

Structure the debate. We've heard debates which were poor because of inadequate preparation. Research is absolutely essential. The debaters have to know what they are talking about! Topics should be of high interest—"Should women be permitted to play major league baseball?"—or of local interest—"Should our town build a municipal skating rink (swimming pool, and so on)?" Be sure that facts are available and that they are used by the debaters.

Radio

We are so accustomed to television as our major source of home entertainment that we tend to take radio for granted. Young people can be given excellent training in listening through the use of the radio. Assign a program and have your class write about it or discuss it.

Another device you might like to use is a combination of radio with recordings. A firm called Radio Yesteryear (Box N-29 Croton-on-Hudson, N.Y. 10520) will send a free catalog listing hundreds of programs suitable for class use. These include adventurous, imaginative programs—such as *The Lone Ranger* and *The Green Hornet.* By listening to the recordings before you play them for the class, you have a chance to develop a series of questions for the youngsters to answer.

How to Work on Speech Skills

Paired with listening, speaking is our major communication tool. Yet, so often, instead of teaching it in our classes, we denigrate it. One learns to speak by speaking, and one learns to speak correctly if one has heard correct speech. It is incredible to hear eighth graders saying "aksed" instead of "asked," "earl" instead of "oil," and "ri cheer" for "right here."

Speaking is taken for granted by many teachers—even very good ones. With this thought in mind, we suggest that you work on this area with your pupils. We've already discussed oral reporting, but let us go into it in more detail.

1. If you ask children to speak, make sure that they are prepared and have something to talk about. It can be excruciatingly painful to try to speak if you have nothing to say.
2. Help your reluctant speakers to think through and organize their ideas.
3. Don't ask them to speak about topics in which they are uninterested.
4. It may be necessary for you to suggest words to them. Many children suffer from insufficient vocabulary development.

Conversations

What problem, educationally, can be more serious than the inability to converse facilely? Yet the number of young people who are unable to do so is surprisingly great. Often these are members of large families, particularly among the disadvantaged. Sometimes an inability to converse is due to shyness. Whatever the reason, if children have problems in this area, they need help. Here are some techniques for helping them:

1. Try buzz sessions. Divide the class into groups, give the groups topics, and ask them to "brainstorm" the topics. Choose topics they'll enjoy, such as "What parents should know about kids." They may do well wiht a topic such as "Karate: What is it? Would I want to learn it?"

2. Try private conferences. Teacher-pupil conferences can help in many ways. They can teach conversation and at the same time help to develop a child's self-image. An excellent way for you to begin these conferences is by saying, "Tell me about . . . ." Then fill in with some experience you think the child has had or would

like to have; e.g., "Tell me about our class trip. Where would you like to go?"

The next point is important. If possible, avoid questions which give rise to one word answers. "Why?" is better than a question which only requires a yes or no answer. For example, ask: "Do you like to watch television? What's your favorite program? Why?"

Many teachers hold conferences about books their students have read. That's fine—providing the youngster is able to read. But often children who have problems conversing can't read either.

It's our opinion that once you agree that the ability to converse is important, you'll see many ways to teach and develop this skill.

How to Teach Spelling

The teaching of spelling has changed little in many years. However, it has often been ignored and, as a result, there are large numbers of people who simply cannot spell. Many college students fall into this category.

If you have children in your classes with problems in spelling, here are methods that we feel can help them. Incidentally, they will work for the rest of your class as well.

There can be no doubt that our language presents difficulties as far as spelling and reading are concerned. Without giving the matter very much thought, we can find exceptions to most of the spelling rules. However, this does not mean that we should ignore the rules. We must approach the teaching of spelling rationally. To do so some materials are needed.

1. A set of spelling books giving the words for which your children were responsible from the first grade until the present. These books are needed to determine the words a child has not mastered on the primary levels.

2. A listing of so-called "spelling demons." These are words which simply must be learned by memory.

Using the first book, do a diagnostic testing. Determine which words the child with problems must learn and begin with those. At the same time, work with words on the current level. The reason for this procedure is that children will learn some words more quickly than others. Words which do not bring a picture to mind often present more difficulties than words that do. In addition to these words, teach the children the words they need in order to write their paragraphs, homework, and answers to test questions.

The system of word study has changed, as we said, almost not at all. However, let us reiterate it here:

1. Decide on groups of words which have something in common; for example, words with the same meaning or spelling (word families, for instance). Using common factors will help the child to remember the words.

2. Write your list on the board and have the children determine the common factor. Give them something to think about.

3. Go over the definitions and discuss the use of each word. This is different from just giving a pre-test, because if you can help the children to see that the word has a personality they will more easily remember it.

4. After you have done these things, erase the listing from the board and give the pre-test.

5. Have the children exchange papers and correct one another's tests.

6. Assign words for the children to learn. You should vary the words given according to the child's ability. Give each child a target. The target can range from one or two words to as many as six.

7. If a child with a problem can learn only one or two words at first, he or she is doing well. Do not expect every child to get all of the words right. If they do, the words are too simple for them.

8. In your listing, you will be working with review words as well as new ones. (The review words were those revealed by the diagnostic test.)

9. If you work with approximately twenty words per week, do not expect to have them all fall into categories. With older children you can use twenty words from one part of speech, but within that category find something else in common.
10. Help the children to learn the words.
11. After the students have learned the words, test them again.
12. When a child has not learned a word, put it on his "Needs to Be Worked On" list. One week out of every five, have the children work on just the words they have placed on this list.

How can children be helped to learn spelling? This depends on how the particular child learns.

1. The author personally learned by writing—writing the word, the chemical formula, the list, and so on over and over again. We used loads of scrap paper throughout school, because by writing we learned.
2. Others learn by listening. We have taught children who need this type of instruction. Using a tape recorder, the child tapes the correct spelling of words he needs to learn. He records the spelling of the entire list and then records it again and again so that he can listen to it over and over. When he feels he knows it, he tests himself by recording the list and writing the spelling of each word.
3. Still others learn by spelling aloud, repeating the words to a teacher, parent, or classmate. Actors and actresses sometimes learn their parts this way—through speaking. This, too, can be achieved with the tape recorder. If a child learns by repetition, this method will help him.
4. Above all, teach the child with problems that he or she cannot possibly learn a word merely by looking at it. Looking is a passive activity, and we learn by actively doing something rather than by being inactive and waiting for the word to penetrate.

Stress the need for correct pronunciation. If a word is mispronounced, it will be misspelled, too. For instance, we have seen the "Star Spangled Banner" written with the following words at the very beginning: "Jose, can you see . . . ."

There is no easy road to spelling. Repetition is often the only way. Nothing can be as discouraging to a teacher as to have to repeat something over and over again and have the child forget from day to day. Yet this happens all the time. In a few cases it may be the result of brain damage or minute learning disability. More often, there has not been sufficient repetition.

When you have a child with problems, don't lose patience with him or her. Instead, give words that he or she can learn. Teach him or her how to study them and then give the youngsters a feeling of accomplishment at being able to do so.

Sometimes teaching spelling rules at the same time that you are teaching lists of words is a big help. However, when you do, *don't teach the exceptions at the same time.* That proves confusing. Allow the child to learn the basic rule and then teach the exception. Don't let the child lose what he has mastered, though. For instance, if you are teaching "ight," include fight, night, might, flight, slight, and so on. Then, at another time, cover bite, cite, and write. Don't teach them all at once.

How to Teach Grammar

The teaching of formal grammar has unfortunately become almost non-existant in this country. We feel that this has caused a lack of understanding of the language—of its structure and function—on the part of many young people. This lack of understanding also causes an inability to communicate, both verbally and in writing. It is with the belief that the teaching of grammar will help the child who has problems communicating that we suggest the plan you will find in these pages.

Grammar is scientific. Basic rules are followed. If our children master these rules they will be able to express themselves far more easily than if they have no knowledge of them. Furthermore, we have found that children enjoy grammar. They can get involved in this work because it offers satisfaction and gratification.

Consider grammar as having two aspects:
I.   The grammar of words (etymology)
II. The grammar of sentences (syntax)

I.   The grammar of words: parts of speech or how we use words.
   A.   All words are divided into eight groups:
      1. nouns
      2. pronouns
      3. adjectives (including the articles)
      4. verbs
      5. adverbs
      6. prepositions
      7. conjunctions
      8. interjections
   B.   To understand grammar, one must be able to decide what part of speech a word is. This depends on the particular sentence and the use of the word in that sentence. For example, consider the following:

   "The train had a locomotive and eight passenger cars." ("Train" is a noun in this sentence.)

   "He will train his dog to obey simple commands." ("Train" is a verb in this sentence.)

   C.   Words change according to their use in sentences. This is called "inflection."

   Verbs change: I go, he goes; I come, he comes.

   Nouns are inflected to form plurals: train, trains; mouse, mice.

II. The grammar of sentences, syntax, consists of two aspects:
   A.   Analysis: taking the sentence apart and determining the part each word plays in it.
   B.   Synthesis: forming sentences. The order in which words are put together is important. The entire meaning of a sentence can change when the order is altered.

   "The Northern Army defeated the Southern Army in the Civil War."

   "The Southern Army defeated the Northern Army in the Civil War."

The position of words determines the meaning of each sentence.

When we teach syntax, we are teaching self-expression so that our students can make themselves clearly understood.

Use of the Cyclical Approach to Teach Grammar

You may begin the teaching of formal grammar as early as the third or fourth grade. However, you should teach it at the level of the children's understanding.

Begin with nouns and verbs. Children grasp the concept of nouns and proper nouns far more easily than other parts of speech. The teaching of this aspect of grammar and spelling (capitalization) at the same time is logical and comprehensible to the youngster.

Techniques for teaching parts of speech are:

1. Have the children each give you a word.

2. List the words on the board, putting them in one of three columns. Don't label the columns, but in your mind make them nouns, verbs, and other words.

3. After each child has contributed one word, announce, "We'll concentrate on this column. Why did I list all of these words in this column?" Have them reason it out. What do the words have in common?

4. After they have worked out the reason (let's assume that is was: "They are all things"), have the class copy the list in their notebooks and add three more "things." This is easy, and it's gratifying. Usually even the slowest child will be willing to do this.

5. Go around the room checking. When each child has finished, put some of the new words on the board.

6. Then announce, "Instead of calling these 'things,' let's call them nouns." Define what a noun is. Next, list more words on the board, each time repeating: "This is a noun."

7. Ask each child to use one of the nouns in a sentence. This way the children hear many nouns used in sentences. Their aural sense is used as well as their visual sense.

8. Then have the children write several short sentences in their notebooks. If the youngsters are capable of doing so, suggest that they write humorous sentences. Review these in class, too.

9. For homework have them write three or four sentences. The following day, have them correct each other's work. (When a child isn't capable of doing so, assist him.)

This technique may be used with all of the parts of speech. Of course, it becomes more difficult with conjunctions and interjections, but it can be very effective.

By requiring the child to think and to reason, you teach him or her far more than if you merely take out a textbook and say: "Read the list of nouns on page 41 and copy it."

Techniques for teaching sentence structure are:

1. Have your children suggest several sentences. Write them on the board. Ask, "Is this sentence clear? What is the person trying to say?" (Have the class put the meaning of the sentence into different words.)

2. Keep going until you get examples of sentences which are not clear. Show why they are not.

3. Offer your own sentences. Show the use of the various parts of speech and the order in which they're used.

4. Have the children change the sentences from declarative sentences to interrogative and imperative sentences. (They'll like this because they usually grasp it readily.)

Again, use the cyclical approach. Begin with simple sentences and go on to more complex ones. (This approach is discussed fully later in this chapter.)

Having the children create sentences and letting the class decide if the sentences are clear and correct is preferable to using workbooks or other printed materials.

Teaching Vocabulary

As you begin to teach new words, indicate what part of speech each word is. Where there are several possible uses of a word, indicate them. Teach the children to use the dictionary to determine this.

Class exercises such as the following are interesting and cause the child who has difficulty communicating to think.

1. Ask the class to list ten words describing how they feel when they receive an unexpected present.

2. Show a filmstrip and ask for a list of words describing it.

3. One teacher working with eighth graders darkened the room, lit a candle, let it burn for five minutes (in total silence), and then asked the class to write down their thoughts.

4. Put the statement "Happiness is . . ." on the board and ask children to list things they think of.

5. Ask, "What's your favorite color?" Have children write it at the top of the page. Then have them list as many nouns as they can which are that color (fully or partly).

6. Use the brainstorming technique. Put a sentence or paragraph on the board. Have the class offer words to complete it.

"I was alone in the house. I heard a knock at the door, but when I looked out of the window, I couldn't see anyone. I heard the knock again. I_____." (Have each child suggest a verb. Begin with the slower children and list the words on the board. The same approach may be used for most parts of speech.)

How to Teach the Concept of the Sentence

As adults, we usually define a sentence as a complete thought, but this definition is very difficult for a child to comprehend. There are many one word sentences—"Stop!" "Go!"—but while we know that the subject of the sentence is "You" (understood), for a child who is unfamiliar with formal grammar, this is indeed difficult.

Before going into more detail regarding sentences, teach the ideas in Figure 6-1 to your children.

Sentences

1. Every sentence begins with a capital letter.
2. a. Every sentence ends with a punctuation mark—a period, a question mark, or an exclamation point.
   b. It is the punctuation mark which tells the person reading the sentence what kind of sentence it is.
   c. There are four kinds of sentences:
      i. A sentence which tells you something. This is a declarative sentence, and it is followed by a period.
      ii. A sentence which issues an order. This is an imperative sentence, and it, too, is followed by a period.
      iii. A sentence which asks a question. This is an interrogative sentence, and it is followed by a question mark.
      iv. A sentence which carries a strong emotional message. This is an exclamatory sentence, and it is followed by an exclamation point.

The same words can convey different meanings, depending on the type of sentence.

Mary hit Bill. (That's what happened. This sentence states a fact, tells a short story. This is a declarative sentence, and it is followed by a period.)

Mary, hit Bill. (Mary is told to hit Bill. This sentence is a command. This is an imperative sentence, and it is followed by a period.)

Did Mary hit Bill? (There is a question about what happened. This is an interrogative sentence, and it is followed by a question mark.)

Mary hit Bill! (This is an emotional statement of what happened. This is an exclamatory sentence, and it is followed by an exclamation point.)

Figure 6-1

As was suggested earlier, teach the concept of the sentence cyclically, too. Cover all kinds of sentences—at the level of the child's comprehension.

After you have taught nouns and verbs, you should teach the concept that a sentence must contain a subject and a predicate. The subject is a noun or a pronoun (or sometimes another part of speech being used as a noun or pronoun). The predicate always has a verb in it. The verb may be only one word, such as runs, jumps, sneezes. It may be two or three words, such as will run, must jump, might have sneezed.

Techniques:

1. Concentrate on nouns and verbs first so that the children have knowledge of what they are.
2. Show their roles in sentences.
3. Put sentences on the board. (Elicit these from the children.)
4. Point out the subject (a noun) and the predicate (a verb). Have the children decide which is which—and why.
5. Elicit more sentences and have the class copy them and underline them. Use a single line for the subject and a double line for the predicate.
6. To teach syntax in greater detail, continue with the object or complement of the verb.
7. Teach the various modifiers of the subject, the predicate, and the object.
8. Continue with a study of the order of words used:
    a. First, in simple sentences.
    b. Next, in complex sentences.
    c. Then, in compound sentences.

This chapter contains a bare outline of a curriculum for the study of grammar. It is hoped by the author, however, that it shows that the subject should be taught and that a simple, rational approach is possible.

How to Correct Sentence Fragments
and Run-On Sentences

A.   Sentence Fragments:

Here, too, we make use of the grammar that has been previously taught. Some sentence fragments do not have both subjects and predicates. If your children can realize that these are missing, they will realize when they are using fragments instead of sentences.

If you teach your pupils to check for the presence of subjects and predicates, they can avoid some types of fragmented sentences.

B.   Run-On Sentences:

The run-on sentence poses other problems. When you are teaching elementary school children sentence structure, we believe that it is best to encourage them at the beginning to write sentences containing one subject and one predicate. As they become more sophisticated, this approach may be changed. However, as they start to construct sentences, they can far more readily recognize sentences which contain simple subjects and predicates.

Youngsters who have never learned to recognize simple subjects and predicates tend to write longer and longer run-on sentences. It is almost as if they do not realize at which point the sentence should be concluded. As you look at their papers you find that they often tend to use the word "then" to extend sentences. For instance, "Mary went to the supermarket then she went home and then she fed her dog."

Teach the children that a sentence is a complete thought when you feel that they are able to understand the concept. Then you can use this definition to show that there were really three thoughts in the above sentence.

Techniques for correcting sentence fragments and run-on sentences are:

1. Elicit sentences from the class. Make sure that you have examples of complete sentences, run-ons, and fragments.
2. Ask the children to write the sentences on their papers and to select the subject and the verb. Then have them decide whether the sentence is:

   complete—write CS
   fragment—write SF
   run-on—write RO

   In each case have them give their reason for the decision.
3. This type of exercise may be repeated many times. Facility in every aspect of language is developed by usage.
4. You may use a reversal of this technique. Have the children write complete sentences and then change the same sentences into sentence fragments or run-on sentences. This technique is good because it causes the children to think and reason.
5. Many textbooks and workbooks are available which give materials for teaching or reviewing various language arts skills.

How to Use Pupil Errors to Teach Functional Grammar

A. Technique

1. Have your pupils write simple three- or four-sentence paragraphs.
2. Select sentences from these paragraphs. (Never identify the pupil whose work is being used.)
3. Duplicate the sentences and have the children:
   (a) Label the sentence—CS, SF, or RO
   (b) Give reason for label
   (c) Correct when necessary
   (d) Select subject and predicate
4. By using the pupils' work, you make the material relevant and you teach the children what they need to know.

By having them correct the work of their classmates, you teach them how to correct their own work and how to do their own proofreading.

B.   Proofreading

You may be able to have some of your students proofread each other's work. This gives you time to work with students who need your time and your personal explanations.

Euclid's famous statement, "There is no royal road to geometry," holds true in language arts as well. While geometry is important to some people, the ability to communicate well is important to every one of us. All of the efforts you expend for your students in this direction are eminently worthwhile.

Chapter 7

How to Manage

Your Classroom Effectively

and Make Your Life Easier

In this chapter you'll find techniques and methods for making your life easier. But may we begin by asking you a question? How do you see yourself? What role have you adopted? If you are able to step away and think about it, we suggest that you do so. Then we have a suggestion. Can you see yourself adopting the additional role of manager or supervisor? If you can see yourself that way—*managing workers*—you may find a much more viable classroom situation for both you and your students.

Management has its own methods, many of which are definitely applicable to the teaching situation. Perhaps it would be easier to divide the work of the teacher into two areas—teaching and running the classroom. There will be times when learning activities, too, require management. However, let's see just how management techniques can be of value.

No matter what method or class structure you use, think of your classroom as a place where many specific tasks must be accomplished. The first problem you have is to figure out which must be done. Remember that you have 30 or 35 eager workers.

They'll do almost any task you ask them to do, and your ability to manage them efficiently will make all the difference in your worklife.

In the classroom, just as in any working situation, when you ask people to do a job you must give them the reason for doing it. You'll find it worth the effort and the time it takes. Busy supervisors often tell workers just to do something without further explanation. Teachers do this even more often. Yet if you explain why you want something done, you'll probably find that the youngster will do a better job because he or she understands what's going on. Giving the explanation makes you seem less "bossy" too. Young people aren't robots, and if you treat them as intelligent human beings you will usually get better results than if you are abrupt with them. If you have an emergency, you can always tell them that you'll explain later. Even if the reason is obvious, take the minute required to make sure that the "worker" understands.

How to Use Pupil Power

Begin by giving every child in your class a job to do. You can make these assignments temporary and then reassign after four or five weeks. However, it is important that *each* child be given his or her particular job. One reason for this is that removal of the job is a form of punishment. There are some youngsters for whom it is difficult to find just the right job, but it's well worth the effort to try. Give each job a title. The word "assistant" should be used if no other more descriptive one comes to mind.

The following list gives some possibilities:

1. Four class officers elected by the members of the class: president, vice president, secretary, and treasurer.

2. Two attendance assistants to record the names of absentees on a list for you and on the blackboard.

3. One blackboard assistant to erase the boards.

4. One blackboard washing assistant.

5. Two clothing closet assistants.

6. Two book distributors.
7. Two materials distributors.
8. Two book collectors.
9. Two materials collectors.
10. Two wastebasket assistants who pass the wastebasket around daily before the class leaves any room.
11. Two bulletin board assistants in charge of displays.
12. Two plant assistants.
13. Two out-of-room assistants who go on errands.
14. Two housekeepers to put things away and to keep the room in order.
15. One filing assistant to file away materials.
16. One or two class librarians to check books in and out of the class or school library.
17. Two "pinch hitters" to take the place of assistants who are absent.

This list is by no means complete. Pupil tutors may also be considered assistants. Other jobs should be created to meet the needs of the class and of the teacher.

The officers, as elected officials, should have important tasks to do. The president should be in charge whenever a teacher is not in the room, help keep order, and assist during fire drills and lead the class out of the building. He or she should also lead the class out during dismissals. The vice president fulfills the president's duties when the latter is absent, takes his or her position at the end of the line during dismissals and fire drills, and assists in keeping order. The secretary should write the class notes on the board and should do the very important task of informing any absent child of the work he or she missed. The treasurer collects all money—for milk, trips, charity, and so on—and keeps records. Before holding elections, describe the tasks each officer is expected to perform. Make sure that any child nominated is willing to accept the responsibility or else does not run for office.

As you see children displaying leadership qualities, you may wish to make them supervisors of the other children. This is excellent providing that they do not become unpleasant or overly zealous in their work. If they show signs of being too bossy, speak to them immediately about this.

It requires time and effort on your part to establish a smoothly running organization, but once you do, many of the tasks you did formerly will be done by your assistants. In an open classroom your students should be made responsible for equipment, including setting it up, as well as for the jobs outlined above.

Give each assistant a feeling of importance. Try to give each some work to do during the course of the day. If possible, don't allow any to rest on their laurels.

Children, like adults, work for rewards. In the classroom the job is often its own reward. Yet, if a class is working well and almost every child is doing his or her job, we suggest a party every so often. Sometimes you might bring the food; at other times allow the class to make it—with you. This is very successful at holiday times—Halloween, Thanksgiving, Christmas, and so on. (When the class "helps" you make the party, they are permitted to bring in food, soda, and so on. You can arrange this by saying: "Would you like to have a party? I'll bring the cake (or whatever you choose to bring). Does anyone want to make a contribution?" Generally the amount of food brought in is far too much rather than too little.)

Stress the idea that the class is a team, of which you are the coach, and that everyone works together. You may use pupils to help other boys or girls to improve their behavior so that the entire team functions well.

Other rewards include notes home to parents. A simple note to the parent is often very much appreciated by both the child and the mother and father. Usually the types of notes sent home by teachers are negative. Here's a sample of a rewarding one:

Dear Mrs. X,
    Johnny is one of our book collection monitors. He is doing an excellent job, and I wanted to share this information with you.

Class trips have proven to be very worthwhile. Here your workers can be of tremendous help.

Be sure that you find the job to fit each child. People have different energy levels, and some children are capable of much more work than others. Also, be careful to avoid creating "pets," since this more than anything else turns children off and creates hostility.

How to Set up Your Room
for Maximum Efficiency

The physical setup of your room will depend on the type of teaching you do. An open classroom requires a setup completely different from that of the structured class. The teacher who uses grouping needs a different physical plant from the one who uses individualized instruction. However, there are certain approaches which will be of help to everyone.

Use your closet space wisely. Have space assigned for books, materials, and clothing. Clean out the space monthly. If you haven't used an item in a month, weigh carefully the chances of its being used again. (Have an assistant do the cleaning out.) Most teachers tend to accumulate materials which they never or rarely use again. These items take up valuable space.

Set up a desk filing system and have an assistant file anything which can be filed—notices, lesson plans, and so on. Keep as few items on your desk as possible.

Set up a filing system—a series of folders—for your pupils' work. Keep samples of compositions, tests, homework assignments, and reports on hand. Give the children the responsibility of keeping their own folders complete and neat. Check them monthly (or have an assistant do so). This serves several purposes. It shows the children that their work is important and is being kept on file. It serves as a check on their progress and is available to be shown to parents.

Incidentally, a fancy filing case isn't necessary. You can use cartons—the correct size can be easily found in supermarkets. Covered with contact paper, these cartons serve the purpose beautifully.

Establish a series of routines and have them written up by the secretary and posted on the bulletin boards. Make them simple and to the point but clearly visible. It's worth a reading lesson or two to be sure that every child understands them.

Decide upon a furniture arrangement and have the children set it up. Do this on an experimental basis. (One highly successful teacher constantly changed the arrangement of the room. The children reacted very favorably.) Of course, the arrangement must fit the needs of the class. A horseshoe arrangement is hardly conducive to buzz groups.

At the close of school each day, have the students put away all materials, replace all furniture, and pick up any litter around the room. Set these procedures up as part of your routines and don't relax them. If you stress the importance of the routines you will find that your work is much easier than it would be if rules had not been established and things were done haphazardly.

If you are not a highly organized person, you will do well to assign the job of desk assistant to a trustworthy youngster. Then he or she can assemble the papers on your desk, sort out various materials, put away odds and ends, and see to it that you always have chalk, an eraser, pens, pencils, and paper on hand. A book rack on the desk is very handy.

Let us add a word about confidentiality and legality. Never allow any child to see confidential materials. Include among these parents' names, addresses, and telephone numbers of the pupils in your class. (Discuss this with the desk assistant. It is not that you don't trust him or her—of course you do—but you are legally responsible for the confidentiality of certain materials. We've known youngsters who abused their positions as office monitors and revealed phone numbers, which led to a long series of crank phone calls.) Don't place temptation in the hands of any child. Keep all records put away in a drawer which the assistant is told is completely, totally, off limits.

How to Train Your Students
to Accept Responsibility

Many young adults complain about the fact that they have never been given responsibility, and when it finally is thrust upon them they do not know how to handle it. Years ago, young people were given tremendous responsibilities at young ages. Sixty years ago it was not unusual for a fourteen year old to be one of the breadwinners, helping to support his or her parents and younger brothers and sisters. Along with this responsibility went respect. Today it seems as if young adults lack both responsibility and self-respect.

It is our belief that even seven and eight year olds may be taught self-respect through responsibility. We have already outlined a series of jobs to utilize pupil power within your classroom. Combine this with additional responsibility for best results.

Each child should be taught exactly what responsibility is his or hers. Be as specific as you can. For example, if you're instructing a child in distributing supplies, it's preferable to say, "Please give each person two sheets of paper," than to say, "Please give out the paper." "Please pile the books in the back of the room" is inadequate. Say, "Please put the books in piles of ten, with the titles all facing in the same direction, on the bookcase at the back of the room." As long as you specify what you want your assistants to do, they know and can follow through. You must remove the guesswork.

Discuss the responsibility. Be sure that the child feels what he or she is doing is important. Telling him or her the reason helps greatly in this regard. Do this not only in reference to jobs but to school work as well.

Be sure that the youngsters accept responsibility for the tasks on which they are working. If they don't, or if they are not aware of what they are doing, the situation is weakened. It's necessary for each child to know what will happen if he or she doesn't carry out an assigned responsibility. Far too often people are excused if they fail to do their jobs. This policy of being excused may cause a pattern to develop—a pattern of failure to live up to responsibilities. It is a disservice to the child. "If you do that again," children are often told, "I won't let you play football." The next time it's exactly the same because the parent is good natured and didn't keep his or her word. It's this type of good nature which can really hurt a child.

You, as the teacher, must teach responsibility. "If you don't return these permission slips by Wednesday, you'll not be able to go on the trip," you tell your class. Then add, "This is your responsibility, and you must assume it." If you are firm in this respect, you do far more to help your students than if you allow them to neglect their responsibilities. It takes more effort on your part, but you are truly doing the child a service when you insist that he or she be responsible for his or her actions. If he or she doesn't return the slip by Wednesday, he or she can't go! This child will remember it the next time—guaranteed!

In the case of your assistants, you should give the youngsters an opportunity to learn the job. You have clearly stated it for them and then actually shown them. If they don't do the job after a fair trial run, relieve them of the responsibility. Discuss it with them but don't give "another chance" again and again. It's a mistake.

In the case of school work, state exactly what the students are responsible for and also exactly what steps you will take if they do not live up to their responsibilities. For example, if a homework assignment isn't done, what do you do? You can give a grade of "incomplete," and when a student gets three "incompletes," a letter goes to his or her parents. The letter should be returned to you, signed by the parent.

You shouldn't pull out your big guns too soon. Use your judgment so that your actions are suitable. Telephoning a parent is stronger action than sending a letter. In some cases, seeing a father is stronger than seeing a mother. (Fathers generally work, and to come into school inconveniences them.)

Follow through! Children truly respect teachers who are firm but friendly. We have seen this demonstrated time and again. They really want to learn, and they respect us for teaching them.

How to Use Pupil Tutors

Pupil power, in the form of pupil tutors, can be highly effective. It saves your time, and also enables some of your students to make use of what they have learned. To use tutoring effectively, here are some hints:

1. Set up the place where the tutoring is to be done so that there is as much privacy as possible. It can be done in the

midst of turmoil, but it's far more effective in a reasonably quiet place.

2. Choose tutors who have shown a mastery of their work. If a child does not understand what he or she is to tutor, the teaching will probably help him or her but be of questionable value to the pupil being tutored. Choose, too, those pupils who are verbal and have the ability to communicate ideas. Generally these are the youngsters who will enjoy doing the tutoring.

3. Use as many children as tutors as you possibly can. This gives you much pupil power and also serves to give ego-satisfaction to many students. You can use tutors to teach small as well as large units of work. Handwriting, for example, can be handled in terms of small units. A child can be tutored in writing the letters "m" and "n" correctly—and this can prove of great help to him or her. (Many spelling errors result from the inability to write those two letters properly. The same is true of "g" and "q." Furthermore, pupils who may not be adept in math or reading may have good handwriting.)

4. When possible, vary your tutors. If you can avoid it, don't have the same children doing the tutoring all the time. Use tutors in such areas as art and sports as well as reading and math. This will help you to have each child serve as a tutor.

5. When should tutoring be done?
   a. During class time. Children can tutor and be tutored effectively while others in the class are working individually and/or in groups.
   b. During the lunch period. We've found that most youngsters are willing to give of their free time willingly. If your lunch room is huge and noisy, many youngsters will be anxious to leave and will work happily with other youngsters. Never leave pupils in a classroom without supervision. We recommend that you keep your door locked (though this will depend on your school's policy) whenever small groups are in your room.

      c. After school. Again, this depends on school policy. We've found that more work is accomplished if the tutoring takes place in school than if it is done at the homes of the students.

6. Supervise! Your active supervision is essential.

      a. You should teach, in detail, exactly what you want the tutor to teach. Go over each item, showing how you taught it.

      b. Give the tutor materials. Include workbooks, textbooks, and work sheets you have prepared.

          Encourage your tutors to use their own ideas and materials as well.

          We've found that in tutoring situations the pupils love to use the blackboards and that even five pairs can do so simultaneously.

7. Encourage the tutors to use their own ideas, too. Make this a creative activity, if possible. Often a change in method will cause a light to show through for a student having difficulty, and we've seen pupil tutors bring in excellent new approaches.

8. Some cautions:

      a. Be sure that your tutors don't miss work that you are teaching to the class. Parental objections have been voiced in this regard, and justifiably so. It is not fair to penalize a child for working with a classmate.

      b. Don't allow any child to become smug or conceited because he or she is doing tutoring. If you note a tendency for this to occur, discuss it immediately with the youngster. If this doesn't help, do not use this pupil to tutor unless you have no one else.

How to Use Class Officers

Time and again we've seen youngsters who are elected as class officers and then virtually ignored by the teacher. This is not good procedure for many reasons. If the class has been asked to elect officers, they should be given the opportunity to follow the leaders they've chosen.

How can you use the officers?

The president should be a trustworthy person who can take charge of the class when necessary. Many times we have seen the class "bully" or loudmouth elected president and the teacher unwilling to give him or her a chance. Yet, when given the opportunity, these youngsters do rise to the occasion. They may have lapses, but who's perfect? However, before you give any child responsibility and before you hold any election, the requirements and responsibilities of the job should be explained. Then, after the election, a private discussion should be held to hammer home any possible causes of failure.

Never ask a class officer to list the pupils who are misbehaving in a class. This causes problems. Instead, have the officer conduct a discussion or place written work left by the teacher on the blackboard.

Have the class officers assist you at dismissal time and during fire drills. Here, too, by showing your officers that you depend on them, you can get better results than if you merely tolerate them.

Set up a system for impeachment and removal of officers. Of course, the option of resignation is open. Never force a child who doesn't want to serve or who is not capable of serving to do so.

Put your class officers in charge of:

1. Parties—permit these often (if school policy is agreeable)
2. Charity drives
3. Fund-raising activities such as newspaper or aluminum collection
4. Behavior on trips
5. Behavior in the auditorium

Class officers may be used to represent the class in the school's general organization, thus eliminating the need for an additional election.

We have found that youngsters can influence the behavior of their peers and that the class officers, backed by the prestige of their offices, often can cause changes for the better. We've asked them to "speak to" other students, and sometimes the effects are very fine. Sometimes they are not quite as successful. However, the method is definitely worth trying.

As we have pointed out before, young people benefit greatly from having been given responsibilities and being able to handle them. You are cheating the class officers, as well as yourself, by not utilizing their services.

How to Train Future Teachers

There are many ways to train future teachers which will add to the successful management of your classroom. You are again making use of pupil power, which is always available and for which the price is right. Furthermore, you give valuable lessons in career education by permitting your youngsters to get a true-to-life sample of what the teaching profession is really like.

Tutoring is one way in which you can do this. Tutoring is usually the most rewarding of the various types of teaching since a one-to-one relationship often develops between the tutor and the classmate he or she is tutoring. We've given instructions for effective tutoring above.

Another way to train future teachers is to allow them to teach groups of children. This cannot and should not be used as a steady diet, but it can be very effective as a "change of pace" and a relatively new experience for the children. *Do not expect your students acting as teachers to be able to keep your class in order.* This is an unusual situation, and the youngsters will tend to be excited and on the noisy side. However, you must be the one who keeps the class under control and who makes sure that work is going on.

On certain occasions you may give future teachers the opportunity to teach the entire class. As mentioned above, this is not good if it is done too often, but certainly this technique may be used from time to time—once or even twice a month. When you are using this method, make sure that the youngster teaching has enough material with which to work. It is so easy for such a "teacher" to run out of material! Here, too, do not think for a moment that the youngster at the front of the room is capable of managing the class. He or she can't as a general rule. We have seen boys and girls teaching reviews and drills of arithmetic very effectively. They can also do a very good job of conducting a "bee"— such as a spelling bee, an arithmetic bee (to drill facts), or a bee for any subject in which you wish to go over material already covered in class. However, you must be actively supervising.

Future teachers can get a great deal out of teaching classes below their grade. Again, they must want to do this—a child participating in this activity against his or her will can hardly do an adequate job of it. Furthermore, the class teacher must supply a very detailed lesson plan. Teaching is not standing in front of the room, scratching one's head, and wondering what to do, which is exactly what we saw one youngster doing. The fault lay entirely with the teacher, who had not helped the child prepare for the situation. *This method should never be used if the teacher is not in the room. The teacher is the one who is in control of the class.* When a young person tries to teach and the class gets out of control, it is a very bad experience for the student.

Would-be teachers often enjoy teaching first and/or second grades. If you are teaching one of those grades, you might want to "borrow" a teacher from the higher grades. You'll find that your children will enjoy the situation. Even if the student-teacher is not very good, the novelty of the situation is appealing. If the youngster is good, he or she can repeat the teaching every two weeks or so. Of course, this should be for a half-hour or forty-five minutes and not more.

How to Simplify Your Record Keeping

We have found that one of the most useful devices for simplifying record keeping is to make up a list of your students at the beginning of the year. Rule a rexograph master, with each name in its own space. Run off this master, and you have it whenever you need to submit a list of your pupils to the office and for your own use.

We have found that using a looseleaf book with a rexographed listing for each marking period can be helpful. We placed notations on the lines for many different items. (This will be discussed later.) Then, when the marking period was over, a new sheet was put into the looseleaf. It literally enabled the students to begin with a clean sheet. It was easier than trying to put little marks in boxes, and it was easier to read. All sheets should be retained until the school term or year is over.

Work out a system which suits you. Many successful teachers mark the positive contributions. "Anyone who answers a question now gets a check," they announce. Then, right on the spot, they put in the checks. I heard one teacher say to a child: "That's terrific. I'm giving you a double check for that." Since the response hadn't appeared out of the ordinary, I questioned it. "That's the first time that boy ever said *anything* in my class. I wanted to encourage him." Isn't that a great idea?

Try to avoid giving "zeroes." If you are able to do so, use the positive approach almost entirely. A check for verbal responses is used frequently. So is "10" or "100." Any such system is fine. Use another indication for homework. We've seen teachers using "HC" for Homework Completed and "HI" for Homework Incomplete. Then, when the assignment is brought in, the teacher crosses off the I. In this way he or she showed the fact that the homework was late but had been done. Select another symbol for class behavior. The letters often used for this are VG, S, F (very good, satisfactory, and failing).

Test grades may be put on the sheet in numerical form, or you may decide to give letter grades instead—A, B, C, D, F. The use of the latter gives you more leeway. An A, after all, stands for a range—usually from 90 to 100.

How to Simplify Your Test Marking

Test marking can really be made simple. There are a number of ways to mark tests. Let's go into them.

1. Having the class mark its own papers is one method we have recommended over and over again. However, there are a number of safeguards that we use. First, no child marks his neighbor's paper. Collect the papers by rows and distribute the papers from the first row to any row but the second. You might

prefer to collect the papers, shuffle them, and distribute them yourself. (This is good as a change, particularly if you use the other method regularly.)

Have the pupils write the test papers in ink. (This may mean that you have to have pens on hand to "lend" them. You have to be on your toes to get them back, or a class assistant or two may help with this detail.) After the test has been completed, all pens must be put away. (This is crucial to the success of this method.) Then pencils come out, and these are used for marking the papers. The first thing you have each child do is write his or her name after the words "Corrected by . . ." at the top of the paper. This immediately makes the child doing the grading accountable.

We have used this method very successfully many, many times. Of course, errors are made. After the papers have been graded, they are returned to their owners and the answers are gone over again. Everyone is looking for points. Hopefully they find several. This makes the procedure very exciting. You will note, however, that you have reviewed the material twice—once while marking and once while reviewing the marking. This is very worthwhile, too.

Make sure that you outline exactly how much each question is worth. If you are testing for factual knowledge, this is relatively simple. With concepts, it can be done, but it is more difficult. One further word: tests with 25 questions are easier to mark than those with 20. The 20 question test gives each question a value of 5 and half credit is 2 ½. This is nuisance. A 25 question test gives each question a value of 4 and half credit a value of 2, which is much easier to work with.

2. You may find that you want to do your own marking—if not all of the time, then some of the time. In that case we suggest that you make up tests of multiple choice questions for which you can use an answer key. Then you can list the correct responses and not have to read long answers. This, too, is educationally valid since many of the standardized tests the children take are of this type and the practice will be helpful. However, remember that such a test may depend on the child's ability to read and that this type of exam may ignore the fact that he or she has learned material but cannot read the questions.

3. Another possibility is the use of marking assistants. We've seen teachers "borrow" students from upper grades to do this work for them. In some school situations this is entirely possible and most worthwhile. In others it isn't. You'll have to check school policy. Is it acceptable to have youngsters miss some of their work to do clerical work for you? (Always assume that work is going on all the time. However, the clerical work you are asking them to do is valuable training in career education and should be approached that way.)

4. Please don't ignore the fact that at frequent intervals the children should be given tests which require them to write paragraph answers. It has been our experience that many children have great difficulty when it comes to doing this. They may be very verbal, but when they have to put their thoughts on paper they are lost. Since writing is an art and develops with practice, we feel that it is urgent that they get this practice.

How to Teach the "Golden Rule"

What has teaching the "Golden Rule" to do with classroom management? A great deal. Basically, it is teaching the children to accept responsibility for their behavior. If you believe, as we do, that we really are our brother's keeper, then you can use this material to teach that concept.

The lesson plan which follows was used with every class in our intermediate school. The anecdote related in it is true and, indeed, was the raison d'etre for the lesson. We can honestly say that there was never a recurrence of this incident or one remotely resembling it. We use this lesson plan every year. Even when the class has had it before, they respond well.

> To: All Language Arts Teachers
> From: M.S. Karlin
> Re: Guidance lesson to be taught on (date)
> Aim: What is the "Golden Rule" and why should we live by it?
> Motivation: Discuss the following material with your students:

We are all individuals. Some of us are tall, some short. Some of us have dark hair, some light, a few are red-haired. Some of us have dark eyes, some light, some in between. What are some other similarities? What are some differences?

Every child looks different from everyone else. No two of us are alike. But some children are picked on by other kids. Why does this happen?

After the discussion, set up a role-playing situation. Have the children act out scenes where a child is being picked on and is "saved" by another child. You may wish to re-enact the following incident, which actually happened to one of our children. This child, a boy, was sitting on the bus, and some girls set fire or tried to set fire to his hair. (Of course, you wouldn't permit the youngsters to use real matches in their re-enactment!) Another boy intervened, took the victim to the back of the bus, and since then has "protected" him.

Next, ask the following questions.

Why should someone set fire to another person's hair or injure anyone else? Why would a person want to do this to another human being?

What should students do about it?

What should *you* (the student) do about it? (Bring out the point that the boy who saved the other boy was a strong, big boy. But even the littlest girl could get help. The bus had been standing in front of the school, so there were teachers available outside the building. However, if the bus had been in motion, the bus driver should have been told.)

Next, role play a scene in which pupils are "shaking down" other students.

Again, question and discuss: "Why do some young people do this?" and "What should *you* do about it?"

Next do a role-playing situation in which a child is hurt when someone running down the hall hits her. (This has happened many times in many schools. Broken teeth are not very unusual.)

Then ask, "What is the Golden Rule?" Elicit it from the children. Have a child write it on the board. Be sure that every child understands it.

Divide the class into buzz groups. Have each group discuss the Golden Rule. Ask the youngsters to figure out why even the perpetrators of "crimes" or unpleasant deeds deserve compassion. Why did the boy defend the kid whose hair was on fire? Why does doing a good deed make the person who does it feel good?

The lesson may run several days, but end it by asking every student if he or she is willing to do one good deed a day—just to feel good. Then ask, "What are some of the things you can do which qualify as good deeds?" Ask the youngsters to write the good deeds they can do on a piece of paper. Title it "Golden Deeds." These should be displayed on the bulletin boards, with or without names.

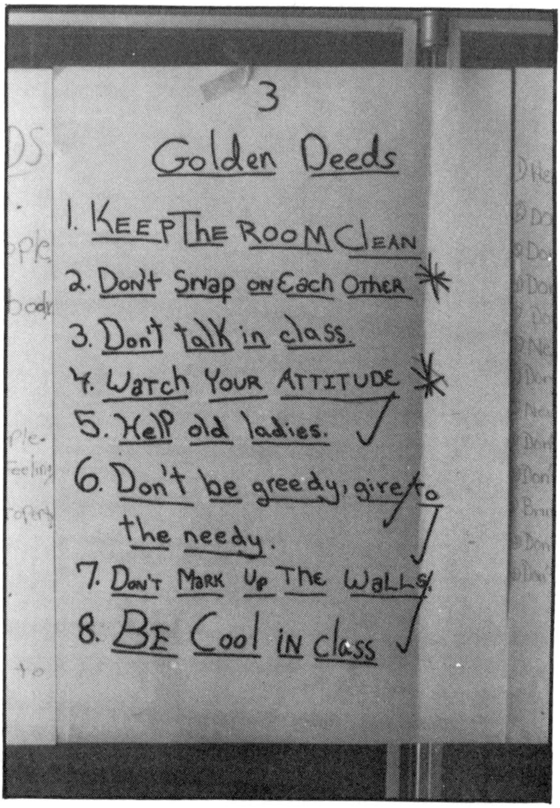

Figure 7-1

Figure 7-2

Please gear this lesson to the level of the children you are teaching. *Stress the internal aspects—that feeling good is something we all want and that this is one way we can feel good. By doing good for others, you do good for yourself, too.*

We honestly believe this to be one of the most important concepts it is possible to teach.

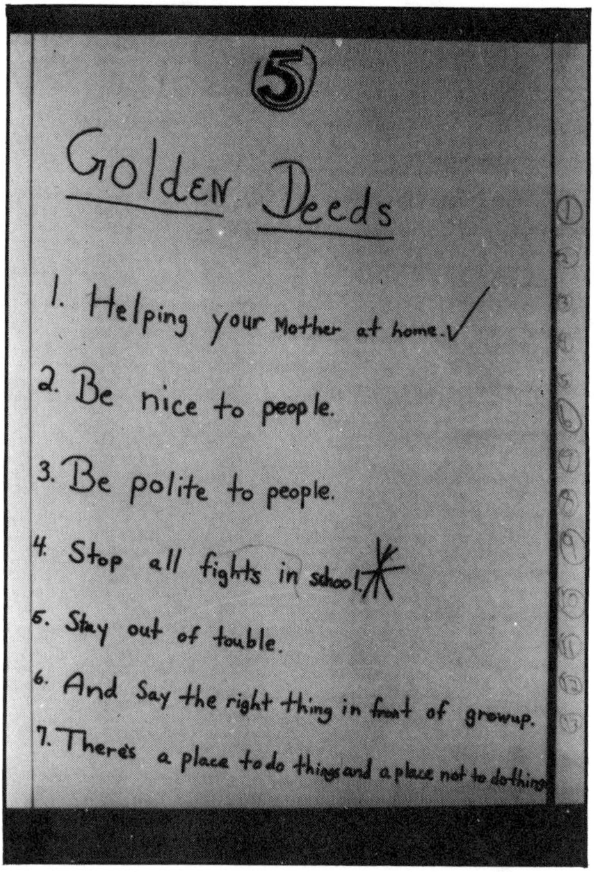

Figure 7-3

Hopefully, you will find many ideas in this book which you will want to apply. If you are willing to try this lesson, we are sure that you'll find that it is one of the best. It was written because the mother of the boy whose hair was set on fire telephoned and said: "Please do something. The kids are always bothering my son." The lesson did help; there was no question about that. But it did far more. We're very proud of it. Teach it—and we're sure that you will be, too.

Chapter 8

How to Plan Your Work

Why Plan?

Planning makes your teaching life simpler. Trying to teach without plans is like going on a journey without any maps. You may wander from place to place, but you don't really go anywhere.

With plans you give a definite structure to your work. Not only do you know where you're going, you know how long it will take you to get there. You will also be able to account for a great many children with individual differences in learning.

With good plans you will never cover your curriculum too quickly. Nor will you realize, with two weeks to go, that you have half of the year's work to teach. These situations won't occur if you have been planning as you go along.

Planning enables you to make teaching a satisfactory experience for you. In industry and career education the concept of job satisfaction is a most important one. There are many teachers who never feel this satisfaction, and one reason is that their teaching lacks planning.

Once you do careful planning, you can make use of your work again and again. There is nothing unprofessional about this. It is not that you are shirking your duty because you want to save time. To the contrary, you are making use of previous experiences and varying these to suit every class and indeed every child you teach.

Your lesson plans enable a substitute teacher to take your place and actually give your class material worth teaching. How often do substitutes waste the time of the children? This is most unfortunate because it need not happen. If you supply plans, you can avoid this problem.

Teachers are often asked for their plans by their supervisors. In some schools having them is a necessity. Even in those schools where this is not true, being able to show good plans will engender a favorable reaction for you from any supervisor.

How to Use Plans Which Will
Be of Help to You

Let's use the analogy of the road map again. Teaching requires a road map. You must know where you are going and how you are going to get there.

"Where you are going" refers to your objectives. Without objectives you cannot teach effectively. How can you decide what your personal objectives are? Your objectives will differ with every class you teach. It's up to you to decide to which you must give priority. Here are a number which you should consider:

1. To teach your students to get along with one another and live cooperatively in this uncooperative world. (This may be called "brotherhood" or "cooperation" or "peaceful coexistance." The name is not important, but the goal is very much so.)

2. To have meaningful, relevant work for each student going on almost all of the time. If one of your goals is to avoid the wasting of time by your students, many of the steps you take would be to satisfy this goal.

3. To get your students to think. Much of what we must teach does not require the students to think—unless we structure their work so that they must do so. Thinking has not been a goal of educators for as long as you might think it has. In fact, it still isn't in many classrooms. Is it in yours?

4. To improve the reading skills of every child in the class. In recent years the emphasis of education has been placed in this area far more than in others. It is our feeling that it still should be and that reading skills cannot be taken for granted. Every skill should be planned for—and taught.

5. To improve the writing skills of every child—including handwriting (the lost art), spelling (the almost lost one), sentence structure, and composition.

6. To develop a love of learning, an interest in the humanities and in the cultures of the past. Here, too, is an area which has been almost forgotten in recent years, but which, hopefully, is enjoying a renaissance. In this area we include appreciation of art, music, other cultures, and all of the attributes which distinguish us as human beings.

7. To bring to every child a realization that the time will come when he or she will have to decide on his or her educational and vocational future and to give each child material on which to base these very important decisions, taking into consideration his or her own propensities and talents.

8. To make learning as exciting as possible so that every child will have a positive reaction to your class and to your teaching. It's painfully simple to lecture to your children, assume they are listening and learning, and then be shocked when they aren't. By striving to make your classroom intellectually stimulating, you bring a verve and sparkle to it which will influence your children tremendously.

These objectives, then, will help you to decide where you are going. They are, of course, long-term goals which can't all be reached in any one lesson but which should underlie the long-range plans you'll be making.

Are you asking: "What about the curriculum? Don't I have to cover that? How do these objectives tie in?" They tie in very closely. Let us say that you are teaching a reading lesson. How can you take into consideration some of the objectives we've listed above?

Much will depend on your choice of reading material. There are any number of short stories which discuss cooperation and getting along with others. Choosing such a short story helps you fulfill that objective. The treatment of the lesson will indicate whether or not you are making the work relevant and meaningful to each child. One way to do so is to put the child into the story. A simple way to do this is to have the children read up to a certain point and then say to them: "Please don't read any further. What would you do if you were in this situation? How would you behave?" After getting the reactions of many, if not all, of the youngsters in the class, say, "Okay, let's see how the author ended the story." This type of "open end" story is very fine for bringing relevancy and meaning to a class. Another way you might handle this is to ask, after reading the story completely, "How do you think you'd have acted in that situation? Would you have done the same thing?"

The type of exercise mentioned above also gets the children to think. Discussion, real discussion, is an excellent addition to every classroom. Furthermore, according to Dr. William Glasser, this is a valuable tool for bringing each child into action. He suggests that daily class discussions be held and that if you give respect to the opinions of the children you will help develop their self-esteem and self-value.

In this particular lesson, what reading skills have been taught? That depends on what you decide to include. It might be a lesson in selection of the main ideas of the story, in reading comprehension, in vocabulary development, or in the use of context clues. The reading skill may be taught separately or as an integral part of the lesson.

This work can be made as exciting and as vital as you wish. Much will depend on the material you select, the questions you ask, and the stimulation you can bring to the class.

Every lesson you teach will take into account a number of these goals, but not all of them. Yet the inclusion of even a few will improve your teaching and make you more aware of the lessons you are planning.

How to Make Plans You Will Be
Able to Use Many Times

If you are teaching the same grade and the mandated curriculum doesn't change, there is no reason why you will not be able to reuse your plans. Not only that, they'll improve from year to year.

We have found the use of a looseleaf notebook very valuable for this purpose. Place each plan on a new page. Use only the center part of the page, leaving a margin on both the left and right sides. For example, if you use 8 ½ x 11 paper, then a 1-inch margin on the left and a 2-inch margin on the right are quite workable.

As you teach a lesson, note on the sides of the pages any questions you develop as the lesson is proceeding, any suggestions made by the pupils, any items you neglected to cover, any references you found after your plans were written, and any ideas engendered by the lesson. You can also indicate in these margins the point at which you stopped if you were unable to complete your lesson.

Date your plans in pencil even though you write them up in ink. Then, if need be, you can redate them for another year's use.

We have found it necessary to list new vocabulary for some classes and not for others and have done this in the margins. It is essential that you make sure, early in every lesson, that the children know what you are talking about. In fact, if a word hasn't been used in your class before, it is worth reviewing the meaning of that word rather than taking the chance that even one child doesn't understand it.

Another advantage of looseleaf plans is that you can keep any rexograph masters in envelopes right in the notebook, along with the plans. This saves filing the masters and then having to search for them later on.

Another use for a file envelope right in the planbook is for clippings. It is amazing how many items relevant to your teaching can be found in magazines and newspapers. Placing them here, where they are readily available, is very worthwhile.

We discovered, however, that looseleaf reinforcements are a

necessity, because after several years pages tear and get lost. You'll be putting a lot of time into your plans at first, and it's a shame to lose them and have to rewrite them.

How to Set up Long-Range Plans

One of the surprises we met was the discovery that not every teacher knows how to write a good daily lesson plan or long-range plan. With that in view, we are going to review the basics of good planning. Remember that we assume that you will be using your plans over and over again and, therefore, that the time you put into them will be worthwhile.

Much of your long-range plan depends to some extent on arithmetic. How much material do you have to cover and in how long a period of time? Very often you are given this information in a curriculum bulletin. However, you may never see this bulletin. Any sort of syllabus may be utilized for this purpose. If worse comes to worse, and neither of the above is forthcoming, use a text book for the purpose. If even that is unavailable, you will have to decide on a series of topics which will make up the year's work.

Study the document you are using and then divide the year's work into workable, logical units. It's convenient to make these units approximately equal in length, but when a topic requires more time than the others you should allot the necessary time. If you don't realize this in advance and the need for more time sneaks up on you, you may have a problem. It's far better to try to foresee this, if you possibly can.

Each unit should have something which binds it together. This will help you in your planning as well as helping the children grasp the material you are teaching. "The New England States" appears to be a better unit than "Alaska, Texas, and Oklahoma," until you realize that the latter is a unit concerned with the production of petroleum.

Work your objectives into your long-range plans since each daily lesson can't contain all of them but each unit can.

Let us assume that you have already divided your year's work into units. Survey each unit to determine roughly how long you will need to cover it. Let us say that you have eight units of work to cover in your social studies curriculum. They are not of equal length, so you allot time to each of them. Since the year has approximately 40 weeks, divide 40 by 8. Then make the necessary variations. (Many curricula are divided into units for you. Then all you have to decide is how much time you will require to cover each one.)

If you are using the "contract" system, your contract will usually cover an entire unit of work, and the time allotted should be that which is necessary for the children to complete their contracts.

If you are not using contracts, you can work your units out by saying: "I need ten lessons to teach this unit. That should take me 2 ½ to 3 weeks." Or you may work in reverse, saying: "I want to take up this unit in 3 weeks. How many lessons shall I divide it into?" Again, study your curriculum or your textbook for help with this. Dividing up the unit will help you in teaching it.

Most people begin their units of work by stating the objectives for the unit. These may be selected from the list given above, selected from the curriculum bulletin, or developed by you. However, they are an important part of the roadmap you are preparing for yourself.

A unit of work should have subject matter which binds it together. This makes it easier for the pupil to grasp. A series of disconnected lessons is far less useful than an integrated whole. Let us say that you are doing a unit on petroleum. You can discuss its discovery, production, and uses. To this you may add the reason for its importance in the world today, the problems faced by nations which do not have it, and careers to be found in the industry.

The unit above has enough subject matter to constitute a year's work or can be covered in three weeks. The difference in length depends on the depth into which you will go while teaching it, the activities in which you will involve the youngsters, and the treatment you will give to the entire subject. You might, for instance, have the class write a *Petroleum Newspaper,* in which all of the information they glean will be put into written, permanent form. This would, of course, require much more time than if you covered the material in a discussion and question period in class.

Another decision you must make is, "Do I want to extend

units of work into more than one subject area?" For instance, much social studies material can be brought into language arts and vice versa. Science is a logical part of a unit on petroleum, and arithmetic problems may be related to it without too much difficulty.

If you wish to use this interdepartmentalized approach, your year-long unit may contain six or eight projects of that type. (You would have to include separate teaching of skills, however.)

Some educators refer to this type of teaching as "organizing centers" or "integrated teaching units." One highly creative teacher, Meredith DeGood, of Columbia School, Peoria, Illinois, used "Careers Around the World" as such a unit.

Writing in *Career Education Workshop,* she states:

> We begin the unit by holding a discussion about world leaders—not just political leaders, but also leaders in entertainment, sports, service literature and education. We establish that each boy or girl will have the opportunity to nominate one person for the class list of world leaders.
>
> Next each student chooses a person who has been highly successful in a specific field of work, and does thorough research on that person and his or her career. Using the material gathered from his research, the student prepares a one-to-two-minute persuasive talk to convince other members of the class that the particular person he studied should be on the class list of world leaders.
>
> Once the list is established, the students each compose a letter notifying the person of his or her selection. In this letter, the student also asks questions about the person's career, and many students request photographs.
>
> An important learning aspect of this activity is locating the addresses of world leaders. The boys and girls may call the library and newspapers for the addresses of syndicated services and use the current *World Book of Facts.*
>
> After the addresses are located and the letters are proofread, the students recopy their letters on school stationery, using the school address for the return address. The letters are now ready to mail; if some are to go overseas, a trip to the post office is in order to determine the correct postage.

Once the letters are in the mail, we clear off a section of the bulletin board for our display, "Careers Around the World." When the replies arrive, the writer opens his or her own mail in front of the class and reads it aloud. We preserve the letter by mounting it in clear plastic film. All answers are put on the bulletin board for the entire class to share. At the end of the year all letters, photographs and mementos are returned to the students.

We have received letters from President Ford, Sir Edmund Hillary, Sandy Koufax, Bobby Riggs, Charles Schulz, Jerry Lewis, Bob Hope, to name just a few.

Here are some of the questions our students have asked in their letters to world leaders:

For political leaders: What courses did you take to prepare you for your career?

For entertainers: Did you ever think you would be so successful in your career? How long have you been entertaining?

Since the people the students write to have such varied careers, the questions are different in each case. Basically, however, the letters cover the following points:

1. They compliment the person on his or her success and explain the reason for writing.
2. They ask questions about the career and whether the person truly enjoys his or her work. Generally the students add a few words about why they are interested in the career.
3. They thank the person for reading the letter, and usually ask for a picture.

The unit has proved to be a great motivator. Each student who receives an answer to his or her letter is so rewarded because he or she has chosen to write to someone in a career he wants to follow.

The student who doesn't receive an answer learns that an unanswered letter brings disappointment. This trains a young person to think and answer all mail.

The unit successfully utilizes English skills (research, letter writing, addressing envelopes, persuasive speaking and evaluating). It has brought to the fore a great variety of careers and broadens the scope of careers available. In social studies it strengthens map concepts as the student explains where and how a particular career is practiced. For mathematics, the postage and cost of the project including the plastic film is always an added factor.

With the current stress on reading skills, the unit is terrific. Doing the research requires much reading. The entire project shows the student the importance of reading and its practical use.

This unit provides exciting times in my classroom. I lose track of how many time a day I hear, "Did the mail come yet?" When a letter comes, the receiver becomes king or queen for a day as a circle of students eagerly waits for the opening of the envelope.

You can use a study of a foreign land as a unit, but don't call it "Study of Mexico." Instead, call it "Mexican Fiestas" and relate the study of Mexico to fiestas. Roberta Schoenbrun of the Oceanside (New York) School System uses embryology as one unit of her curriculum with fourth graders. (This is described in *Classroom Activities Deskbook for Fun and Learning,* written by the author, published by Parker Publishing Company, 1975.)

Your choice of units is limited only by your imagination. People, sports, travel, literature—all of these can be the basis for exciting units of work.

How to Set up Daily Plans

As you set up your daily plans, keep one question foremost in your mind: *What are the children learning today that they did not know before they came to school and that they will benefit from knowing?* We have found, after years as a supervisor, that even well-educated teachers with long years of experience can forget this fundamental question. We watched one gentleman teach a lesson on Amos the Mouse to sixth graders. It was charming but without any real value. As a supervisor, I ask myself about every class I observe: "Are the children learning something they did not know before and is it of value to them?" Of course, teachers must do review lessons to reinforce learning, but even then it is my personal feeling that material should be included which is new and relevant.

With this concept in mind, that it is essential that *your children learn,* we approach planning on a daily basis.

The following plans may look complex and time-consuming, but they will be of tremendous help to you. They will be your guidebook, your resource, and your security blanket (when you need one). They'll take time, but you can use them again and again. Ms. DeGood, whose unit we cited earlier, has used it for many years.

Parts of a Lesson Plan

Motivation
Aim
Concepts
Activities
Materials Needed
Thought-Provoking Questions
Individualization
Summary
Assignment

Now let us examine each of these parts in detail.

A. Motivation

This is the "key to the city"—the beginning of the lesson and the point at which you "hook the kids." It is your motivational device which will gain and hold their interest.

What are some motivational devices? They range far and wide—from an anecdote you tell to the class to a filmstrip which intrigues them, from a record you play for them to a film you stop in midstream, from a controversial statement you write on the board to a newspaper clipping you read to them. Whatever it is, your motivational device should be the beginning of your lesson.

B. Aim

The aim of the lesson is really the point you are trying to put across, the item you are trying to teach the youngsters, the skills you are developing with the children.

One of the more recent developments in education has been the use of behavioral objectives. A behavioral objective is a statement of what the individual child is to be able *to do* as a result of the lesson you have taught. For example, the pupil will be able to recognize the prefix "trans," define it, and list five words containing it.

But be careful, because the aim of the lesson tells you exactly what it is you must teach. If you say, "The pupil will be able to recognize the sound 'ph' when it appears in twenty different words," you have your work cut out for you.

C.   Concepts

This section is very important, because it is here that you state all of the material you wish to cover. This may be a substantial amount or a very small amount, depending on the work you are doing and, of course, the grade level of the children you are teaching.

List the points you plan to make. All of them. Don't take them for granted.

Sometimes this section will be brief, as in a skills lesson. Sometimes, particularly when you are teaching a series of ideas, it will be a list for you to check off and points of summary for your class to enter in their notebooks.

D.   Activities

This section is the meat of your lesson. What are you going to have the children actually do?

Many lessons consist of discussion—of question and answer. There is no doubt about the importance of this technique as a teaching tool. However, it should never be considered a replacement for activities which the children actually do. We suggest that you make it a practice to include in every lesson some activity which the child performs himself or herself. Even if it is reading and answering questions in writing, it is preferable to discussion in class because in discussions often half of the class participates and the other half "woolgathers." Even with spirited discussion going on, we have observed numbers of youngsters not really "with it."

Activities may be anything from using worksheets to working in notebooks, using Task Cards to holding a debate, having children report to the class on their research to planning and executing a class newspaper or a class bulletin board. Many of the activities listed below, in the homework section, may be used in class as well.

E. Materials Needed

At this point in your plans, list the materials you will need for the lesson. If you are using the text, indicate the pages. Make this section a guide, too, which will help you as you go through the day.

F. Thought-Provoking Questions

There are many people who feel that this part of the lesson will develop as you teach the lesson. However, it has been our experience that if you have prepared from five to eight good questions, your teaching will be simplified greatly. While planning, you are able to sit quietly and think up questions which would not come to you while you are speaking. Many questions undoubtedly will, but thought-provoking questions are different. They have to reflect your ideas. Questions requiring simple factual answers are not thought-provoking, whereas the "whys" and "hows" generally are. Questions such as "If you had been in this situation what would you have done?" or "How do you feel this could have been improved?" are far better.

G. Individualization

In virtually every class there are children who will not receive maximum benefits from the classwork because it is either too difficult or too simple for them. Include the work for those youngsters in your plans at this point.

Decide for every lesson what you want and expect each child to learn. This helps you to establish your guidelines.

Individualization is especially needed in teaching skills. Detailed methods of individualization will be found later in this chapter.

H. Summary

Do not neglect to summarize your lessons in the form of notes which you give to the class. Summaries reinforce learning and show the youngsters what the main points of the lessons are. The tests you give should come for the most part from these notes.

You can, if you choose, use the notations you have made in the "concepts" section of your plan or you may find it more effective to write an additional summary in terms of specific points.

I. Homework Assignments

Every lesson you teach should be backed up by a homework assignment. However, telling students to study certain pages for a test is not nearly as effective as selecting the most important points covered and asking the students to write two or three sentences explaining each.

The variety of homework assignments you can give is tremendous. Here are some key words and phrases which you can use to begin a number of assignments: Test; explain; define; compare; diagram; find out how; find out why; create a game; write a sentence describing; write a paragraph describing; illustrate; create a mural; create a play; create a montage; design an experiment; create a poster; find examples in a magazine, in a newspaper, on the radio, or on television; consult two (or as many as you deem necessary) references for information about; make up_____examples to show; go to the library and find out.

This list is only the beginning, and its purpose is to orient your thinking toward different, thought-provoking homework assignments.

How to Individualize

We've already mentioned individualizing in terms of lesson planning. One method which may suit the needs of your class is the contract method.

Constructing Contracts

A contract is a unit of work which is prepared in a specific fashion. It contains a number of lessons and lasts for a period of at least several weeks.

Within the contract there is first an introduction and then a listing of primary objectives. This is followed by a list of resource materials which the child may use—including filmstrips, maps, photographs, books, films, and encyclopedias. Next, there is a list of additional activities from which the child may select those he or she is interested in completing.

The list of primary objectives would include a variety of activities. Each child would be expected to complete two-thirds of them; however, the brighter children would be expected to complete all or almost all of the objectives. (Many children who are not expected to do so complete almost all of the objectives.)

The objectives involve doing different types of work. Let us assume that your children are working on a contract involving social studies. Here are some possible objectives:

1. Draw an outline map and indicate on it the following places: (ten to fifteen places would follow)

2. Write a paragraph describing the climate in _____ .

3. Write the pages of a diary of a person living in _____ .

4. Describe and draw a sketch of two animals living in _____ .

Following a list of references are the additional objectives. These might include writing a play, creating a game, doing a montage, preparing a talk describing the religion in the area being studied, and constructing some of the musical instruments used in this area. The contract is an excellent device for children who are able to read on grade level but not as good for those with reading difficulties.

Using tests for diagnosis enables you to individualize your instruction. Again, you must first decide on the material which you expect every child to learn. (It is unrealistic to expect each child to learn every piece of information covered.) Having decided which information you think everyone in the class should learn, you then teach it. Next, give a test. After grading the test, you have a diagnostic tool which will tell you which information was not learned by which children.

As soon as you have this information, you can reteach the material the children need to learn. While you are doing this, the children who have already mastered the material should be working on other assignments. In this way you can be sure that every child will come away with some knowledge. Not all of them will come away with everything, but it is unrealistic to expect that. You may be surprised at how much your "average" children will have learned.

Never reveal this system to the class. As far as they are concerned, you expect them all to learn everything. If you indicate that your expectations for some are less than for others, you'll find the children will work less hard.

How to Group

Using the system outlined above, you can group *according to the information you have to reteach.* If more than one child needs to be retaught a topic, establish a group and teach it to them. Make your groups flexible and change them as often as the material being taught changes.

Groups are often used when skills are being taught. If you teach a new skill to the entire class, some of the children will grasp it far more quickly than others. Establish groups; then assign other work to the group of children that has mastered the skill, while you work with the group that has not. In this way, the time of the children who learn more quickly is not wasted.

Chapter 9

How to Obtain Materials

at Little or No Cost

How to Send for Free Materials

There is a vast variety of materials available at almost no cost whatsoever.

The United States Government Printing Office issues books, booklets, and newsletters on more topics than you could ever think of. For a list of these topics, write to the Superintendent of Documents, U.S. Printing Office, Washington, D.C. 20402, and ask to be put on the mailing list. (You may have to make several requests; we have found that one is not always enough.) The list that you will be sent will include materials that cost nothing or only a minimal amount. Frequently you will receive a bulletin which gives the titles of the latest publications and instructions on how to send for them.

These materials are excellent. They are simply written and are perfect for planning lessons and class use. There is a wealth of material on consumerism, most of which is free. It's worth checking to learn what is available on any topic you plan to teach.

Various departments of the Federal government have publications to offer, and these are usually sent free. The Department of Agriculture, for instance, has a great deal of material which is useful for teaching science.

Many private industries publish excellent teaching materials. General Electric, for example, offers a variety of publications. You may write to their Public Relations Department, Schenectady, New York. The best lists of free materials are to be found in two books: *The Elementary Teacher's Guide to Free Curriculum Materials* and *The Educator's Guide to Free Guidance Materials*. These books contain lists of films, filmstrips, slides, audiotapes, videotapes, scripts, audiodiscs, and printed materials, including charts, bulletins, pamphlets, exhibits, posters, and books. The sole cost to you is postage, including return postage for some of the materials.

These books are published yearly, which is very important for two reasons. First, you are more likely to get the materials you request if they are listed in the current guide than if you are working with an older one. Second, you will want material which is as up-to-date as possible. We have used these guides for many years and have never been disappointed. All of the materials have been well worth the cost, time, and effort involved to get them. The beauty of these guides is that any teacher, in any school, even with the most limited funds, can have the latest materials available for the cost of the guides and the postage. I have found that student secretaries can do the actual work of sending for the materials, thereby giving them valuable secretarial experience and saving the teacher's time. The guides are available by mail for $9.75 each from the Educator's Progress Service, 214 Center Street, Randolph, Wisconsin 53956.

Many teachers have found that membership in the AAA (the American Automobile Association) is very worthwhile for them, because, in addition to the road service offered, the AAA also has available for its members, gratis, excellent materials for the teaching of the geography of the United States. The Tour Books are particularly fine, and they cover every state of the country. Maps of all sorts are available free, and even the advertisements for the tourist attractions of the various states can be used by the creative teacher.

For career education there is a great deal of information regarding where to send for free materials in the *Occupational Outlook Handbook*. After each section describing a career, there are usually several organizations listed to which one can send for further information. The students can gain valuable experience writing letters in addition to receiving career information if you have them write for it. A child interested in learning more about becoming a librarian would find the following organizations and their addresses listed: American Library Association, Special Libraries Association, Division of Library and Educational Facilities, Bureau of Libraries and Learning Resources, U.S. Department of Health, Education and Welfare, Washington, D.C.; Secretariat Federal Library Committee, Room 310, Library of Congress, Washington, D.C.; and American Society for Information Science, 1140 Connecticut Avenue N.W., Washington, D.C. 20036. The *Occupational Outlook Handbook* is available from the Superintendent of Documents, U.S. Government Printing Office, Washington, D.C. 20402, for $6.85.

Another source of materials which many teachers overlook is parents. One of the science teachers in our school was interested in setting up a radio station. Funds were short, and he appealed to the parents through the Principal's Newsletter. He received some of the equipment necessary, and it was possible to buy the rest. Another teacher, seeking to set up a class library, had her pupils write letters to their parents requesting contributions of books. There were many books forthcoming. Another teacher asked for cuttings of plants, which the children then planted. The results were beautiful, and the youngsters enjoyed watching the plants grow. Seeing that some of the cuttings didn't "take" was an experience which was beneficial for them as well. Still another parent contributed cardboard tubes on which fabrics had been rolled. The art classes were able to create fascinating totem poles using these tubes. In a home economics class, another parent contributed scraps of felt, which were made into a striking mural. Old toys were collected, repaired by the industrial arts and home economics classes, and then distributed to needy children.

The Federal government has proven to be a source of materials for a number of schools through its surplus property program, which is operated by individual states. To discover whether your state has such a program, contact the Federal Property Office in your state capital.

How to Use Teacher-Made Materials

Like most teachers, I used to make stencil after stencil, year in, year out, until I realized that if I kept a file of these, I could reuse them. Even if the stencil had to be recut, the model was there, and time was saved. Furthermore, I discovered that certain of my students could do this type of work more efficiently than I and were delighted to do so. It was a learning experience for them, and I was able to turn to other tasks.

The next discovery I made was that other teachers made stencils. By pooling our resources and setting up a file, we found that we often had a stencil on hand for whatever topic we were teaching. We then began making other stencils to create variety, and these, too, went into the file. In that way, we could use our own work again and again.

The principle of reusing your materials is important. Whenever anything you have done is successful, file it for future use. You build up your materials and your bag of tricks. You need both!

It takes a great deal of time to write up either task cards or contracts, and there is no question but that these should be used again and again. Of course, you'll want to make additions and changes, but the basic work has been done.

There are certain teachers who have developed projects which are highly successful. We know of one teacher, for example, whose Christmas trees, made of digest-sized magazines which were spray painted and decorated, are a school tradition. Remember that anything a child has never seen or done before is new to him or to her, although you may have done it year in and year out.

There is no need to reinvent the wheel—and it's possible for you to benefit from other teachers' work. There are many books which can be of help to you in this regard, a number of which you may be able to find in your school library. The various "Teachers' Guides" which accompany many of the text books can also be used. Much of the material put out for the bicentennial can be used by the inventive teacher for years to come.

Use as many of the creative arts in your teaching as you can. Bring in drawing, painting, sculpture, montage, metal work, wood work, and photography, and blend them into every unit you teach. You will find that your work is more interesting, and the youngsters will be delighted. We've found that making dioramas and stage settings is a great favorite, and by saving some of those which were made in previous years, you can have excellent samples to show to the boys and girls.

How to Use Pupil-Made Materials

We still have in our school a model of the Shakespeare theater at Stratford-on-Avon which was made by a young man as his gift to our school. Today he is a practicing physician, but he is always remembered as the boy who made the theater model for us.

Does your school have a magazine? Why not use that in your language arts class? Children love to read material written by their peers. We've found that excellent motivation.

We have found that many children are anxious to earn extra credit. By giving additional assignments involving bonuses, we had a plethora of charts and bulletin board displays. With the advent of felt tip pens, chart making has been simplified considerably.

One huge favor you can do for your children is to insist on excellence. Never give that bonus unless the work is worthy of it. (Of course, the complexity of the material should depend on the intellectual level of the child. However, never accept any chart which has an error on it—in spelling, content, or anything else.)

Occasionally, you can assign specific charts. We recently had, at Prall Intermediate School, a "Pride in Prall" contest. The charts which were submitted were hung everywhere in the school. They were successful in helping to develop pride in the school, and many students won prizes for their work. (The prizes were boxes of candy which cost us 60¢ each.) These charts will be kept in a file until next year—when they will be used to motivate next year's contest.

Charts on any subject can be made by your pupils—and should be retained in your chart file. They can be used on your bulletin boards to motivate your classes in the future.

Figure 9-1

Figure 9-2

Games and puzzles may also be constructed and used time and again. If you have facilities for laminating them, so much the better. However, this is not a necessity.

We have found that youngsters are anxious to "leave legacies" to the students of the future. One teacher said to her class, "These games will be here long after you have gone on to high school—and even to college." She said this on a Friday. The following Monday fifteen more games were brought in—many representing a great deal of work. They were based on the class's study of electricity and magnetism.

Figure 9-3

Your youngsters can and should make sets of flash cards for both spelling and arithmetic. We have found this technique to be very effective for the teaching of "spelling demons" and number facts. Each child should make his or her own set of cards while in class, following your instructions.

Use 3 X 5 index cards. If you must economize, they may be cut in half. Have the children write an example on one side of the card in this manner: 6 x 8 = ? On the other side of the card have them write 6 x 8 = 48. Do this for all of the number facts.

To use the cards, the youngster places them in a deck with the question marks all facing up. Then he shuffles them, and they are ready for use. The child sees the first card. It reads 3 x 5 = ? He figures out his answer. It is twelve. He turns the card over to check. He sees that the correct answer is 15. He therefore places the card, question mark up, in the back of the pile. He runs through the entire bundle of cards. Whenever he answers one correctly, he puts that card aside. He will repeat the ones he has missed until he has learned them all.

This procedure may be followed with all of the multiplication tables or with only some of them, depending on the children's level of learning.

To use flash cards for spelling, have the child write or print two spellings of the same word, one correct and one incorrect, on the same card (e.g., "eror" and "error"). Then, on the reverse side of the card, have the child print only the correct spelling. In this way it is easy to identify the misspelling since it will only appear on the card as one of a pair.

The procedure we have outlined is followed by each child alone. Children can also work in pairs, following the same procedure. Each child uses his own set of cards, and the child who has discarded all of his cards first is the winner.

How to Use What's Dead and Buried in the Bookroom

Every school we have ever worked in or visited has a bookroom which contains materials the creative teacher can use. Furthermore, most supervisors are delighted when the stuff is used, and, honestly, there are uses for it. However, don't advertise your visit. Speak to your supervisor quietly about this and then go in yourself to investigate. If you are accompanied by other teachers, you will have to share the spoils.

Old textbooks—no matter how old—are sources for photographs which can be used to make excellent scrapbooks. One teacher was known for her use of old books, which would have been discarded otherwise. She had asked her colleagues to send all old books to her. Each year her class cut up the books and made scrapbooks related to some topic they had studied. For instance, one book was on "People the World Over." (Photographs from other sources, such as *National Geographic* magazines, plus occasional ones taken by the parents of some of the students, added to the interest of the scrapbook.) Other topics for scrapbooks included flowers, trees, minerals, mountains, and faraway places.

Another use for old texts is for making task cards. Often there is material at the end of each chapter which lends itself to this purpose. Paragraphs, plus questions on them, may also be used for making task cards.

You can often find enough material *on different grade levels* in the bookroom to construct your own individualized reading program. This will take time, but you will find that you are able to use the program for years.

Select, from old books or magazines (or even standardized tests *if you are permitted to use them*), reading selections of varying degrees of difficulty. Prepare a file folder for each. Use oaktag, cut to approximately 8 ½″ x 11″. On the outer cover place the name of the selection. Open the folder and paste the reading selection at the top of the left-hand page. Below it place the vocabulary you feel should be introduced. Make sure that every word the child must know if he is to comprehend the selection is included in this list. (Adjectives, for example, do not usually fall into this category.) On the other side of the folder place a series of guide questions and below that a series of activities. These activities might include the following:

A. Doing a sketch, making a drawing, or representing something from the story by creating a symbol.
B. Writing a paragraph on some aspect of the selection.
C. Researching some aspect of the selection.
D. Writing "a day in the diary" of one of the characters.
E. Preparing a playlet of one scene in the selection.

Offer a choice of activities. In order to indicate the reading level, you can color code your material by using different colored felt tip pens to write the titles on the front cover.

You'll need a set of at least as many folders as there are youngsters in the class to begin your program. You'll find that you will want to add more as you use these.

Old copies of "Teachers' Guides" can often be found in the bookroom, and these, too, contain ideas and materials you can use as part of an individualized program and in planning your lessons.

If you can find novels or short stories, you can use them as part of your class library. Establish the library, incidentally, knowing that some of the books will disappear. If they go into children's homes, that isn't so terrible, is it? Of course, you'll request books from parents, since they are sometimes another good source of materials (depending on their economic situation).

Look for dictionaries, and, if possible, try to find one for each youngster. We have encouraged children actually to read the dictionary—and found that some enjoy it. A dictionary is a resource that they should always have available.

Some bookrooms contain maps, globes, flags, scientific models, charts, and equipment which would be far more useful in a classroom than in a closet. Children are naturally curious—and placing a model (without any explanation from you) in class can engender intellectual curiosity.

Keep your eyes open. If you have materials in the building, why not make use of them?

How to Use Newspapers and Magazines

Both newspapers and magazines can be used by every teacher in almost every classroom. Papers such as *My Weekly Reader* bring current events to the youngsters at their level of comprehension. Other, similar publications are equally valuable. *Read* magazine, published by Scholastic, has proved to be terrific with classes of unmotivated students, and we have found that it has changed their attitude toward reading.

The daily newspaper can be a very valuable tool. Because children have a shorter attention span than adults, long, involved articles are not good. However, short articles on a variety of topics can be used for many purposes.

1. Use articles as part of the material in your individualized reading program, following the steps outlined above.

2. Introduce the various features of the newspaper— international, national, state, and city news; editorials; human interest stories; sports. Discuss the different types of special interest materials—from "Dear Abby" to the stock market, from bridge to fishing. Try to interest your students in reading the newspaper daily.

3. Offer credit for each article brought in related to a topic your class studied. (If you discuss the presidency, Congress, the governor of your state, and the mayor of your city, you can "open the door" for making many articles relevant.) Set up bulletin board displays and have each article stapled on it in an appropriate place. Have this display changed frequently (have your bulletin board monitor do this). Old newspaper materials turn yellow with age and look as if they are years old.

4. You can use the local newspaper as a guide for establishing your own school or class newspaper. We have found that this is good motivation even with slow classes. Brighter children love it. Use interviews as a source if there is a dearth of news in your school.

Magazines may be used in much the same ways as newspapers. We sometimes use articles for teaching materials—duplicating them for entire classes. Many times a point can be made more easily by having the class read it from a magazine.

Do you have "reluctant readers"? Try giving them copies of *Sports Illustrated* or *Hot Rod Racing,* movie magazines or *Ingenue.* Encourage your students to contribute magazines to the class library. (Check them out first. Most young people have an innate sense of dignity and would not even consider bringing unsuitable materials into school. However, this is not true of everyone.)

Comic books may be considered, as we have already suggested, supplementary reading materials. There are commercial ones produced for school use—King Features' *Popeye,* with text devoted to careers, is an example. Others, too, may be satisfactory. Check them out before you use them.

One use of newspapers or magazines which you may enjoy is using them as "history recorders." Each time an event of importance occurs, put away a copy of the newspaper that deals with it. You can place the paper in a plastic bag and seal it to prevent deterioration. We recently saw a series of *New York Times* dating back to 1941 which a teacher had saved and used as motivation for much classwork. It is worthwhile to save the entire newspaper rather than merely the front page. Insight into the life and times of a period can be gained by reading old newspapers or old magazines. They provide a dramatic way to show the changes in the cost of food and other essentials of life.

How to Obtain and Use Book Publishers' Samples

Most school administrators receive a large number of book samples which you can put to excellent use. They are fine for giving you teaching ideas, supplying models for charts, supplying photographs, and supplying tasks for task cards. Probably their most important use is as resource material which your children can use while doing projects.

Attendance at meetings of educational organizations is one way to obtain a great many samples. Publishers are anxious to bring their wares to the teachers and administrators who will ultimately purchase them. Signing up for sample copies requires a little time and effort on your part, but the results are worth it. If your supervisors plan to attend such meetings, ask them to sign up for samples of texts for you.

If you are using a textbook which you particularly enjoy, why not write to the publisher for a catalog of that company's books? You can then request copies of the books you hope to purchase. Many times we have purchased the books we've sampled, a fact which we have brought to the publisher's attention.

Check with the central office of your Board of Education. Some teachers report having been able to obtain sample copies through this office. One particularly successful coordinator holds book fairs once a year in her own district. Various publishers are invited to exhibit—and rarely is an invitation turned down. Many sample copies are distributed—and orders for books subsequently placed.

Sample copies of books may also be given as prizes. Novels, anthologies, and biographies are suitable for this purpose.

How to Create Books for Use
in Subsequent Years

We have already mentioned the fact that our students enjoy writing "for posterity," and we have used this for motivation many times. This applies to school magazines which are printed professionally. It also applies to anthologies put together by individual classes.

Most classes have some talent—and with your encouragement, plus a great deal of effort, a substantial book may be developed.

Here are some suggestions:

1. Hold a brainstorming session to select a theme. Try to find one which will attract many of the youngsters. (It's very difficult to come up with one in which everyone can become involved.) Possibilities: A. Our favorite— people, places, games, things, or activities. B. If I could become anything in the world, I'd choose to be . . . C. Jokes, funny stories, and riddles. D. History in the making.

2. Try to get a contribution from every child. This is no easy task, but it is worth the effort.

3. When you have enough material, suggest to the class that each child try to illustrate one of the selections. Next, have each youngster read his or her work aloud and the class decide on who will illustrate it.

4. Have each youngster write his or her contribution on a rexograph master. (It must be *perfect*. Not even one error.) Suggest that the parents check this work. It will get them involved and save you much time and effort.

5. After the masters have been run off, have the children assemble and staple the pages together.

6. Have one child design a cover which can be hand colored and have each youngster do this for his or her own book.

One very fine book was produced on the topic of careers. Each 6th grader researched a different career and wrote up the research. Another class did one on "Transportation," and another did one on "Our City."

The writing of children's books is an interesting project which some youngsters enjoy. The book may be the result of one child's work or may be a joint effort. An added incentive can be the fact that the books may be sent to book publishers for consideration.

Chapter 10

How to Prevent or Cure Classroom Chaos

Every person who has been teaching for any length of time will probably agree that teaching is different from what it was ten years ago, or five, or two, or even one. There are profound changes going on in society which have been occurring since the end of World War II, and these have had a tremendous effect on children. Many of these changes are beneficial, such as the demands and ultimate changes resulting from the "black revolution" and from the "women's liberation movement." The climate in our classrooms, however, is a constant reflection of the social changes going on and is therefore of a restless nature. Because so much of the family structure as we knew it is different, the youngsters we teach are different. The changes have made a teacher's work more difficult than ever before.

Gone are the days when the teacher was automatically respected as a figure of authority. The fact that a person is a teacher does not mean that he or she will get respect from all of the children. Some of the youngsters will accord respect, of course, but by no means will all of them. Many of our pupils have not learned respect for any person in their lives before entering the classroom and therefore cannot transfer it to the teacher. The deference you get today as a teacher you have to earn, and this is no simple matter.

Our youngsters are questioning. Even those who come in with respect for their teachers are not satisfied with pat answers.

People who are not in front of a class have no real concept of how truly difficult it can be. Some years ago, my editor asked me to review books by other authors—educational books. He was anxious to have me do this, he said, "Because you're on the firing line." I resented the remark and used to argue about it. No more. We in the schools *are* on the firing line. While I no longer actually teach a class, I do actively take charge of a lunchroom with five hundred youngsters of all races, creeds, and colors. Our intermediate school age group (grades six to eight) is among the most difficult to work with. These children are in a transitional stage between childhood and adolescence, and they're in action all the time. I write this to prove that I'm in there and not up in an ivory tower. The techniques, methods, anecdotes, and stories that you read in my writings are all true. Names and places are sometimes changed, but the basics are all right out of my experiences or those of my colleagues.

How to Establish Yourself as "The Teacher"

As we said before, you will not be given the "respect" you may think you should get as a matter of course, and you'll have to earn it. How, specifically, do you earn it?

1. Be firm. Think about your class, set up your rules, and then stick to them.

Don't establish rules which are unnecessary or not meaningful. For instance, there are some teachers who get very upset if a child eats while in class. Yet, if the youngster is hungry, isn't eating the intelligent thing to do? You have to speak to the child to explain that he or she should eat breakfast. (We've found not eating breakfast to be the cause of most eating in class.)

If gum chewing bothers you or is against your school rules, don't permit it. But if you aren't upset by it—why make a fuss?

Rules that involve respect for other children's persons or property are essential. No class can function without them.

Being firm is very important. If you say that you'll do something, you must do it. Idle threats are out of the question. We all know the tale of the "boy who cried wolf." It is doubly valid in the classroom.

Let us say that your class is disorderly and you have to waste time quieting them down. "We'll use the beginning of your lunch period to get this work done," you announce. Then you recall that you have an appointment. If you don't keep the class, the next time you make the statement no one will pay any attention to it.

Using part of the lunch period to make up work missed has proved a successful technique for some teachers.

2. Do not accept noise or disruption. From the first day, if there is one child who does not cooperate, talk to him immediately. Talk to him quietly and personally, but don't ignore him (or her). If you don't take care of problems from the start, the next day there will be two or three youngsters disrupting—and in a week no one will be interested in working quietly.

Probably the most important advice we can give is this: Think of yourself as being the manager of this team. If you can get the team members to work with you and to be anxious to please you, you've got half the battle won. (I use this strategy with 500 youngsters. It's not foolproof—but it works most of the time! Remember that you are in charge, and every child must know it.)

We've seen different techniques used to teach youngsters self-control. There are some teachers who never have to raise their voices, whereas others do. One of the most successful methods we've seen is a change of pace. This technique involves speaking softly for the most part but occasionally, when warranted, changing the tone completely—and blasting.

Make work a privilege. One lesson we observed brought this idea home to us. The class had been divided into reading groups. "If you can't cooperate, you won't be permitted to read," the teacher announced. I expected the attitude of the youngsters to be, "Who wants to read, anyway?" I couldn't have been more mistaken. The girls and boys were most anxious to read, and their cooperation and participation was excellent.

The strongest tool you have to work with is interest. If you are able to make your lessons intriguing enough to catch and hold your children's interest, you will experience far less difficulty in the classroom. Bored children become discipline problems. Reaching every child isn't easy—but it's worth the effort.

Probably the first step you should take is the establishment of routines. If routines have been established, the children's need for security is satisfied.

How to Develop and Establish Routines

Have you ever seen a class enter a room, sit down, and begin work? You'll agree, I'm sure, that it's a beautiful sight. It is well worth working toward this goal.

Begin by working out a signal which you will use to get everyone's attention. We've seen a variety of signals. One teacher clapped her hands whenever she needed the class quiet. One of my colleagues whistles shrilly. Still another teacher raises her hands. My favorite technique, although it has drawbacks, is to flick the lights on and off. This is effective if the class has been doing group work or any other work which causes a din of conversation. The drawback is that occasionally a youngster may flick the switch, causing a moment of silence, and then a loud groan on the part of the other children.

No matter which signal you think of or decide upon, make sure that you explain it carefully and stress the need for instant compliance. Explain to the class that emergencies arise frequently and that if everyone cooperates there is far less danger to everyone—students and teachers. Do not allow any child to make a game of this or treat it lightly. The training of your class to respond to such a signal will be of value to you in a host of different situations.

Decide on the exact manner in which you want your children to enter your classroom. Will they be permitted to enter individually or in groups, or do they enter as part of a line? Do you want them to sit down until they are told to hang up their coats or hang up their coats as they enter the room? Think this through, decide, and then teach the class the routine.

Try to be flexible. Any routines that you set up should be subject to change if you or the children think of better alternatives.

Remember that the routines (and self control procedures) that you establish in the beginning will be of tremendous help to you in May and June.

Routines for distribution and collection of materials and books, for boardwork, and for individualized work are necessary.

Routines are good because they develop a sense of security which children (and adults) need. They alleviate anxiety and can do much to prevent chaos. If, for example, your children have learned the routine of entering the classroom and sitting down to work, you have most of them settled. Then, if there are a few who require your attention, you're able to give it to them.

Expect the youngsters to follow the routines and don't accept the behavior of those who "forget." Speak to them, but always be willing to give them another chance.

A good system to further motivate the class is to have a "routine party" once a month. (Maybe on the last Friday of the month or on the first of the month, but always at a specific, "routine" time.) However, the party is a reward. If there are one or two children who do not cooperate, warn them. If they change, fine; if not, tell them that they will be excluded. Then, if necessary, send them to a supervisor. Remember—never threaten if you cannot follow through. And never reward bad behavior.

How to Use a Parent Telephone Campaign

Many children (far more today than even three or four years ago) will test you. The very youngest, who have never had anyone say no to them, will behave the same way in school as they do at home. You will almost certainly have to say no to them. (If you don't find it necessary, you are unusually blessed.)

In spite of the fact that they may not exert parental control, parents do want their children to be successful in school. We have found this to be true 99% of the time—although we've dealt with our share of hostile parents. However, no normal parent will ever say that he or she doesn't want his or her child to learn. We often begin interviews by saying, "We both want the same thing for your child. We want him (or her) to do as well as he (or she) is capable of doing."

Your first contact with the parents of children who show lack of self-control will probably be by telephone. To prepare for this, on the first or second day of the term have each child write his name, address, and telephone number on an index card. This saves you from having to look this information up. Keep the index cards handy, and inform the children that you will be in touch with their parents, if necessary, and that "I have the phone number right here."

Telephoning parents can have many benefits. You can call to comment on both positive and negative behavior. However, let us begin with the latter case.

When you telephone, as when you interview a parent in person, begin by saying something good about the child. This can be difficult, but there has to be *something* good about this child, and you have to find it. Your purpose is to get the parent to feel favorably disposed to you, and nothing does this more quickly than if you say, "Your son is a very intelligent boy." The parent swells with pride. It would be cruel to burst the bubble, so you do it with tact by saying: "But I need your help. He hasn't been doing his homework, and it will slow down his progress. I know that you don't want that to happen." We use this approach all the time. It works beautifully. The actual pattern is as follows: Begin by saying something favorable. Continue by stating the difficulty as tactfully as you possibly can. Then ask for some action on the part of the parent. Don't ask the impossible, but request help which can possibly be forthcoming. End by thanking the parent and restating, "I know that if we work together we can do a great deal to help your child."

If you feel that your telephone call isn't succeeding, ask the parent to come in to see you. In other words, don't take no for an answer. While it is true that there are some parents who have very little influence on their youngsters, most will try, and the child, seeing that you mean business, is often impressed by the phone call. (This is exceedingly effective on the high school level.)

Never allow your call to seem trivial. If a child is slipping in his or her work, the parent has a right to know, and most parents are very grateful for the time and effort you exert on behalf of their child.

If you are calling on a serious matter, such as an incident in which the child hurt another child or himself, you may want to reach both parents (if the child doesn't live in a broken home). Calling in the evening will possibly enable you to talk to both parents or to learn if there is a father living in the home with his family. (Knowing that there is no father gives you insight into the family situation which can be valuable to you.)

The telephone campaign technique involves calling the parent of every child who is in any way disruptive. It may take you several hours at first, but the number of homes you must call will diminish rapidly as the term progresses. If you would like to use this device to regain control of a difficult class or to help specific youngsters to develop self-control very rapidly, here are the steps to take:

1. Announce to the class: "We have a great deal of work to do. Everyone must cooperate if we are to get it done. Therefore, I would like you to know that if I find you are not cooperating, I will telephone your parents *today*."

2. Continue with the work. If there is any child who doesn't cooperate *to the fullest,* telephone the parent that afternoon. (In homes where there is no telephone, write a letter asking the parent to either telephone you or come in to school to see you.)

3. While you are speaking to the parent, using the dialogue suggested above, tell the parent that you will call again the next day if need be and ask if that is all right with him or her.

4. Don't go back on anything you say—ever.

This method is not foolproof, but it does work in many cases.

Be very professional in your telephone calls. This is not a buddy-buddy situation—this situation calls for dignity and concern. Don't talk too long, and make sure that the parent realizes that the matter is serious.

You may wish to call for a number of other reasons. If a child is out sick, you may wish to call to find out what is the matter and to give the parent the work the youngster is missing. Parents are very grateful for this type of attention.

How to Use a Letter-Writing Campaign

Another form of communication which you may wish to use is the letter or written note. (A letter is generally mailed; a note is taken home by the youngster.) These can be excellent devices from the public relations aspect.

Recently, two of our young ladies were involved in a terrific battle with hair pulling and punching. After it was over, one of them had a huge lump on her forehead. We called the parents of both girls into school. When the mother of the girl with the lump arrived, she looked familiar. We discovered that she had had another daughter in the school (who had a different father and consequently a different last name). At that time, she had been in for frequent conferences and had been very hostile. This time her attitude was entirely different, and we wondered why. Her comment to the girl gave us the key. "After all those nice letters I've been getting about you, why did you have to go and spoil it now?" She had, indeed, received many letters from her daughter's teachers as part of our campaign to give credit where credit is due, even if it is only for what might be considered relatively minor details.

Handwritten notes are extremely effective, and many are treasured by parents long after their youngster has graduated from the school. However, if you wish to, you can use a form letter, such as the one reproduced here. It was originally written by Mr. Robert Pisano, now of Tottenville High School, Staten Island, N.Y., while he was a teacher at Prall Junior High School.

Anning S. Prall Intermediate School
11 Clove Lake Place
Staten Island, New York 10310

Norman H. Harris, Principal

LETTER OF COMMENDATION

Date_____

Dear Parent,

Your (son, daughter) should be commended for the fine work (he, she) has exhibited recently in (his, her) reading class. The specific areas in which your child showed outstanding ability are listed and checked off below. If you have any questions or comments about the reading program at Prall, please feel free to communicate with the school.

Sincerely,

Reading Teacher

_____ 1. Improvement in reading comprehension
_____ 2. Outstanding classroom cooperation
_____ 3. Excellent class participation
_____ 4. Outstanding Book Analysis Sheet
_____ 5. Excellent class notes/notebook
_____ 6. Participation in special class project or program
_____ 7. Work done beyond the required class assignments
_____ 8. Excellent vocabulary work
_____ 9. Other _____

Approved: Mrs. M.S. Karlin
Assistant Principal
Language Arts Department

If you must write a negative comment, be accurate and not judgmental in your attitude. The letter below was developed by a number of teachers, and they have found it helpful.

Anning S. Prall Intermediate School
11 Clove Lake Place
Staten Island, New York 10310

———————

Dear Parent,

We are well aware of the fact that you are concerned with your child's education. We know that you will cooperate with us in regard to the matter indicated below.

Please forgive the use of this form, but it requires far less time than writing a letter, and I do want to be able to give parents this information. If you would care to speak to me, I would be happy to set up an appointment. Please drop me a note telling me when I can reach you.

Your child has not:

———— completed his class work

———— done his homework

———— been paying attention to classwork

———— been coming to class on time

———— been in class for the last week

———— done passing work on the last two tests

———— done his/her book report

———— shown respect for his fellow students or teacher

Other comments ————————————————————
————————————————————————————
————————————————————————————
————————————————————————————

Due to the above reasons, your child is not doing as well as he/she could do. I hope that you will speak to ———— about this and take the proper measures so that your child will not lose valuable instruction. Please sign this letter and have your child return it to me.

Sincerely,

—————————————

Teacher's Signature

—————————————
Approved: Norman H. Harris, Prin.

* * * * * * * * * * * * *

I have read the above notice about my child's school performance.

| ———————— | —— | ———————— |
| Child's Name | Class | Parent's Signature |

Never put into writing anything that you cannot substantiate. You should not *say* anything that you can't prove either, but *writing* it can be deadly. If there is a serious problem, don't write it—instead, ask the parent to come into school to speak to you.

Commendation letters should be issued whenever a child deserves to receive one. Placement on the Honor Roll, for example, should be accompanied by a commendation letter. Don't be stingy with commendation letters. We have found them to be excellent motivation and, as mentioned above, a very good way of communicating with parents on a highly positive level.

How to Use Parental Conferences
to the Best Advantage

Parental conferences are one of the most important tools the teacher has at his or her disposal. Many school systems schedule these several times a year. We have found it almost axiomatic, however, that the parents you want to see are the ones who never come in during conference periods. You can try to get them to come in by writing short notes, telling them: "I've set aside time to see you on _____ at _____ a.m. If that time isn't convenient, please get in touch with me by note and let me know when you can see me without causing disruption to your schedule."

Use the first parental conference to find out as much as you can about the child. You can usually learn much by asking, "Would you like to tell me a little about Jackie's early life?" This usually brings forth the information you want. If it doesn't, you can lead into it. Ask about physical health, siblings, and outside interests. Try to make contact with the parent. (We have found this to be of absolutely inestimable value when problems develop later on.)

In any conference, be as positive as you possibly can. Never antagonize a parent. Remember how emotionally involved with the youngster he or she is. (When parents come in for a conference, we always offer them coffee. Rarely do they accept. One day a parent explained, "I couldn't drink anything now—I'm so upset.")

In any conference, try to give concrete examples of what it is you are talking about. If a child is quarrelsome, have him or her write a paragraph about an incident which will reveal this. (Usually youngsters behave in very much the same way at home as they do while in school, but not always. There are some who are terrors in school and angels at home, but they are relatively rare.) If the child doesn't finish his or her work, the problem can be shown very easily. Whatever your complaint, try to have evidence of it.

Remember that because parents are emotionally involved with their children, they want to help them, and if you can offer them suggestions in this regard, they are very grateful. The very worst thing in the world you can do is be negative. Some teachers will say to a parent, "Your child shouldn't be in this class." Wrong! If the placement is wrong, the person to see is the supervisor and not the parent. Above all, don't antagonize parents. It's bad for them—and for you.

How to Use a "Do Now" to Begin Your Class

As part of your routine, the "Do Now" can be extremely valuable. Train your class to respond to the words "Do Now" by taking out a sheet of paper and a pencil and preparing to do work. As soon as work is written on the board, they are to begin to do it.

What is a "Do Now"? Briefly, it is work which requires the youngster to write and to think. It should not be "busy" work but, rather, valuable material from which the child will benefit as much as from any other work. It is of relatively short duration and is reviewed and graded immediately—thus offering immediate gratification. It is kept as part of the notebook, and the material covered shold appear on quizzes or tests. Many teachers place a "Do Now" on the board for the class to begin working on as soon as they enter a room. If you have a volatile class, this is one way to get them settled down immediately. If you give credit for the work done, it is possible to get every child to work. It is also good because it sets the tone for the day.

This brings up the situation where a child announces, "I have no pencil." You may wish to have pencils on hand which can be purchased by the forgetful students. (It is surprising how many children have money with them.) You may wish to have a monitor who is in charge of lending out writing implements. If they have no paper, we suggest that you give it to them if you can. However, this should be done quietly and without fuss or muss. If a child constantly appears without the materials he or she needs, a telephone call to the parents often helps to remedy the situation.

You may use the "Do Now" to review the work you covered the previous day, or you may use it for reinforcement of skills. Another type of "Do Now" is vocabulary development; for example, you may have the children suggest words relating to a particular topic, such as "List five words describing how a person may feel," or "List five ways in which rain affects living things." The listing of possible "Do Nows" is truly endless.

How to Use Written Work for
Quieting Down a Noisy Class

There are certain times of the year, such as right before Christmas or summer vacation, when most teachers find that their children are in a highly excited state. And there are times when teachers don't feel as well as they normally do. These are the times when written work can be used to great advantage. It can also be used when there is a full moon and when, for no reason whatsoever, the kids are off the walls. (If your classes are never in this state, please accept our sincere congratulations and, if you like, skip this section.)

Children need to realize that the education we are giving them will be of help to them some time in the future, when they are called upon to earn their livelihoods. Therefore, if you want to do a large written-work project which is of value, relate it to the future. For example, every person must know how to spell, and, therefore, a written review of the rules of spelling and the so-called "spelling demons" is worthwhile. Many teachers, when they want children to have information, will duplicate it and distribute it to them. This is unnecessary. Instead, write the material on the board and have them copy it into their notebooks. You may have difficulty with children who are unable to write well, but you can get the majority of the class working and then help the rest. Stress the importance of the material they are writing so that they realize its value.

You may choose to have the class write a review of the term's work (effective before Christmas or before summer vacation) covering every important concept studied.

The rules of punctuation, the basic ideas contained in any historic document, such as the Constitution or the Bill of Rights, or a review of the most important concepts studied in arithmetic are all worthwhile.

A vocabulary list of words with definitions (or without definitions so that the class can look up the definitions) or rules of phonics (for those classes requiring them) will provide excellent material.

After the youngsters have copied the list (and the work required to copy accurately is not wasted) give them a short-answer test on it. This can then be marked by changing papers and having the class do the actual grading. (Point out that every question will come directly from this material and that, therefore, if they study the material, they will get 100%).

For those children who do not have the ability to complete the work, have your more capable children assist them after the latter have finished their own work.

Written work of this type requires a great deal of preparation on your part, but you will find that resources such as the *World Book Encyclopedia* can be an excellent source.

The emphasis that you place on the importance of the material you are giving to the class will influence the success or failure of the technique. It is within your power to make it work well for you.

How to Use Behavior Modification

Stated in its simplest form, behavior modification involves rewarding appropriate behavior and ignoring inappropriate behavior. Let us say that you have a youngster who is constantly calling out and who refuses to stay in his seat. To use behavior modification techniques, you would not acknowledge any contribution he made unless it was made when he was given the floor. If he called out, you would ignore it completely. You would also ignore anything he did while inappropriately out of his seat. (This is very difficult to do, but with this technique you would attempt it.) However, you would reward him for staying in his seat. Rewards may take the form of comments, such as saying privately to the child, "Jim, you are doing your work beautifully today," or to the class, "Jim, your self control is improving, and we are very proud of you." (You would make such remarks to other youngsters in the class as well. If you commented only to Jim, you would probably antagonize the others.) Rewards may be commendation letters to the parents, "smiling stamps" on the child's work, or placement of the child's name on the chart of "Classroom Helpers," which you have posted on the bulletin board in a very prominent place.

Daily grades can be used to modify behavior, too. Use a daily report card, with space for your initials and for the parents' signatures. Many parents who are not very involved in their children's schooling respond well to this device. In our school it is called a "Conduct Card," and the children are given one for periods of one week.

If you set out to try behavior modification with a particular child, inform the parents, telling them exactly what you are doing and why. "Jim has two habits which are interfering with his progress," you tell the mother. "He calls out instead of raising his hand, and he gets out of his seat and runs around the room occasionally. I am trying to change this behavior by rewarding him for doing his work without getting out of his seat and for making his contribution to the class without calling out." There is a reason you should let the parents know what you are attempting to do. One mother said to a teacher, about two weeks after the teacher had instituted this program, "I am so glad Jim is doing so well. He says you never yell at him any more."

Behavior modification works with certain children. Others, however, are not affected—especially since they often get the "acclaim" they are seeking from their classmates. It will work well in a class in which the rest of the group is anxious to work. If the disruptive child receives no support from his peers, he often changes in response to this technique.

How to Use the Guidance Approach to Help the Youngsters Develop Self Control

Let's define the term "guidance approach" first. In using the "guidance approach," you try to help the youngster understand his own behavior and, more important, the reasons for it. There are many children who have no close personal contact with adults (not even their parents) and have little rapport with anyone other than persons their own age. Others don't even have that. In using the guidance approach, you offer this personal contact and interest, and you provide the opportunity for the child to talk about what is troubling him or her.

Your basic tool is the conference, interview, or rap session— the name given it is unimportant. What is important is that you set aside the time to speak to the child quietly, on a one-to-one basis. Some of the most successful sessions I have had with youngsters have been over a Coke after school or even over a sandwich during lunch hour.

If you are willing to accept the concept that the child who has not developed self control has not done so for very good reasons, and you try to ferret out the reasons with that child, you can be of help to him or her. Many children do not understand what the entire concept of self control means. They have grown up in situations where it's "every man for himself," and they function the same way in the classroom.

If you have a youngster who is giving you difficulty, your first action should be to take the child aside and speak to him about his behavior. Do not chew him out or yell. Instead, speak softly, and ask him to tell you about himself, his family, his former experiences with school, his friends, what he does for recreation, and so on. Learn, if you can, if he lives with both parents or if there has been a broken marriage. (You will be shocked at the large number of children who come from homes where there is but one parent.) When you have a picture of this child, you can proceed to work on the reasons for his particular type of behavior.

We are not attempting to give you a full course in counseling in this chapter, but you will see a pattern emerging after you have interviewed a number of children. Now, how can you reach them? You can attempt to show them why they are important human beings and why their school work is important to them—in terms of their future lives. They need arithmetic skills, for example, in order to buy the things that they will need. They will need to be able to read signs, instructions, and newspapers. Use this type of discussion, asking them why they will need an education. Get them to contribute as much as possible and have them do all of the talking if you can. (Another thing sooner said than done. Some children are relatively uncommunicative, and you'll have to "pull teeth" to get them to take an active part in this process.)

Most of all, establish yourself as a friend. Then offer a plan of action which the child can accept or reject. Work out methods for him to use on an hour-by-hour basis. Do not work in terms of things which will happen next week. Talk about today. When the youngster has been successful for a day, go on to the next day. As he is able to see himself doing well, he builds self confidence and usually, along with that, self control.

Your secret weapon is close, personal contact—something which many children need desperately and from which they can benefit immensely.

How to Keep Your Children Gainfully Employed

This device is so simple that you'll love it—and it takes little energy and effort on your part once it has been established.

What is it that we want our children to be proficient in more than in any other subject area? Your answer will probably be reading. So much stress has been placed on reading that it is second nature for us to give it primary status.

Children learn to read by reading. Therefore, set up a library of books and magazines that your children *will want to read.* That sentence contains the clue to the success of this technique. The books can be from the library, but they must be attractive and must be on subjects the youngsters find interesting. Check with your librarian for such a selection. Then include magazines, but screen them carefully.

Set up this "library" and tell your youngsters, "After you have completed your work, you may read any material you choose from the library." If you have been successful in the selection of the contents of the library, your children will be gainfully employed reading for much of the time. You can help them to develop a love of reading in this way, which is worthwhile and can serve them for their entire lives.

You may have to search for materials. Some of the publications of Scholastic—such as *Read* and *Scope* magazines—are very fine, and they will hold the interest of many of the youngsters. Other magazines may be about sports and automobiles. (You can use "adult" magazines, but be sure to screen them.) There is interesting material for even the slowest learners, but you'll have to look for it. *Sports Illustrated* and *National Geographic* magazines are good for some classes. Even comic books are worthwhile, if you can get the permission of your supervisor. (Get permission before you use them and, again, screen them carefully.) These are easy to obtain since the children will be glad to bring them in.

Anthologies and thin books are good for your slower children since they will not be intimidated by them.

No one can object to children reading, and by making it a reward you place a high value on it. We recommend this technique very strongly. Even if the materials disappear, you are achieving a goal—helping develop an interest in the printed page and a love of reading.

How to Break up a Fight

It is regrettable that a topic of this nature should have to be covered in a book of this type, but fighting is a fact of life among some children. Children fight. (After a professional boxing match, particularly one which is highly publicized, many youngsters will engage in bouts of their own. These often begin "in fun" but may become serious quickly.) How can you break up a fight? Here are some steps to take:

1. Send for help. Send any other child nearby for assistance. It is far easier to break up a fight if there are two adults than if there is only one.

2. Scream! Many youngsters hate the sound of screaming. "You screamed right in my ear," one child fairly shrieked at me. But he stopped hitting the boy he had been pounding.

3. Move any other children away. Often innocent bystanders get hurt. Other children should not be standing close by and should be chased from the vicinity.

4. If a second person arrives, each of you can pull one of the participants away. Your aim in all of this is to prevent anyone from being hurt. This includes yourself.

5. If you are alone or if you must do so, pull the hair of each participant. This method usually works with immediate results. If one's hair is pulled, the pain is intense, and he or she usually lets go of the other person. We have used this method with amazing results. However, do not go into the middle of the fray unless you feel one of the participants will actually hurt the other. We've had to get into fights because one child had the other in a headlock, and the victim looked as if he would be choked very quickly. There was no time to wait for help. Fortunately, situations as serious as this arise rarely, but one should know what to do when they occur.

6. Women must be extremely careful since blows to the chest area can cause serious problems to develop.

Repeat! Your first procedure is to send for help. If you must act because there is a child in serious danger, then and only then, step in and pull the hair of both participants. (Don't do this if you do not see serious danger.) You must judge the seriousness of the situation, and no one can say you *had to* break up the fight. You have a method for breaking up fights, but use it only if you feel it is almost a matter of life and death.

Chapter 11

How to Deal with Disruptive Children

Every human being responds better to love and kindness than to anger and impatience. No one enjoys being screamed at or being ridiculed, and yet these things happen to children every day—and they are perpetrated by teachers who consider themselves to be gentle and good-natured. However, we are faced with a dilemma, because youngsters often confuse kindness with weakness and a soft voice with a weak will. The answer lies in being firm but friendly and with keeping your word. Each time you say that you will take a specific action and you do not take it, your effectiveness is cut immeasurably. With this in mind, we suggest that you handle your youngsters, and particularly the disruptive ones, with affection and a very strong will.

Let's begin by taking a close look at the disruptive youngster. We can list many reasons why children are disruptive. However, in this book we are stressing solutions to problems, and with that goal in mind, we will try to give you many of the techniques which we have found to be effective when dealing with disruptive children.

We try to differentiate between the hyperactive child and the disruptive child. Hyperactivity is sometimes caused by a medical problem, and the hyperactive child should be examined by a physician as part of your plan to help him.

Disruptive children are generally more hostile and angry than hyperactive youngsters. What causes his or her anger? is the question you should ask yourself in regard to any disruptive child. If you can determine the answer to this question, you have an indication of the point at which you should begin your work with him to dispel some of the anger.

Here are some possibilities:

1. The child can't read and the work you are covering is beyond his comprehension. He becomes frustrated and then refuses even to try.

2. The child has no strong parental influence and has grown up without ever having had any. Therefore, he has a total disregard for authority. He resents you for exerting even a minimal amount of authority.

3. The child has been the victim of indulgent parents. He enters your class feeling that he is "king of the mountain" and can do as he pleases. If you try to stop him or make demands on him, he rebels.

4. The child has a very short attention span and cannot stay with any activity for any length of time. When you try to get him to do so, he becomes defensive.

5. The child has developed the attitude that he can't ever do anything right. This failure syndrome makes him bitter and rebellious.

6. The child is physically uncomfortable. One reason for this may be that he is hungry. Many children do not eat any breakfast and suffer from low blood sugar. They don't realize they need food, but they behave unpleasantly.

7. The child craves attention and will go to any lengths to get it. This youngster can be very disruptive because his need is so great.

8. The child has significant emotional problems. These children should be handled by guidance counselors and psychologists as soon as possible. A child who attempts

to cause physical pain to himself or other youngsters falls into this category.

Your first step in dealing with any disruptive child is to have a private conference with him after a specific incident has occurred. If the incident was of a serious nature, the interview should be on the same day if possible.

"You just did a very serious thing," you say to the child. But you say it without hostility. "Do you understand how serious it was? Why did you do it?" Depending on the response and the ensuing conversation, you should be able to tell something about the reason for the child's behavior.

"You cannot behave this way in this class," you tell the child, again without anger. "I would not allow anyone else to behave this way, and I cannot permit you to do so either." *It is essential that the child realize that you will not tolerate that behavior pattern by him or anyone else.*

Explain to the youngster, "I want you to do well in my class. Do you want to?" Most (not all) youngsters will say yes. Then try to work out a plan with the youngster which will enable him to be successful. Give him an opportunity to achieve some positive results. This can make a world of difference.

In what way will this plan help with the types of youngsters we've listed above? In the case of the child who can't read, your plan will include specific work in that area. In the case of the child who has no understanding or respect for authority, you have to explain to him or her exactly what you're trying to do to help him or her learn that respect and why he or she must learn it if his or her adult life is to be successful. Obeying laws is part of the responsibility of every person living in a democracy, and a respect for authority is one aspect of obeying laws. It is necessary to teach the same material to the over-indulged child, who also does not respect any authority.

In the case of the child with the short attention span, your solution would be to include activities of short duration at first and then include activities requiring attention for longer and longer periods of time. Children need to achieve success, and every child will benefit from activities which are structured to make him feel successful. An example of a success-building activity is the following: Every child can cut out photos and put together beautiful montages; this is an effective project that you can use with the child who feels that he can't do anything right.

Social workers can often help with children who have problems such as physical hunger. In most schools your referral would be to the guidance office or to the administration. When brain damage is suspected or when you suspect emotional problems, these cases, too, should be referred for help.

How to Use Behavior Modification with the Disruptive Child

No matter what causes disruptive behavior, your first step should be refusal to accept it.

At the very first sign of running around, calling out, or any act which disturbs the functioning of the class, immediately make it clear that this behavior is unacceptable. Calmly, quietly, but firmly, let the child know that the behavior is not acceptable.

If the behavior continues, a private talk with the youngster is certainly the next step. If the child is disruptive but not dangerous to himself or to others, you can explain that you will try to ignore him if he is uncooperative, but that if he is willing to try to cooperate you will be delighted to acknowledge good behavior.

You must remember, however, that there are some 30 to 35 other youngsters in your class and you cannot reward some without rewarding others. We've seen very successful teachers use ingenious devices for rewards. One permitted children deserving of the honor to write letters requesting materials, which were sent to the writer at home. The letters were written in class, on school stationery, with the postage paid by the school.

The need for a good "reward" prompted three teachers to get together. They decided to hold a "film festival." They used the *Educator's Guide to Free Films* and obtained the use of excellent films for the price of the postage. Then, every two weeks (on Friday) they showed one film to those students who had been cooperative and had completed all their assignments. The first Fri-

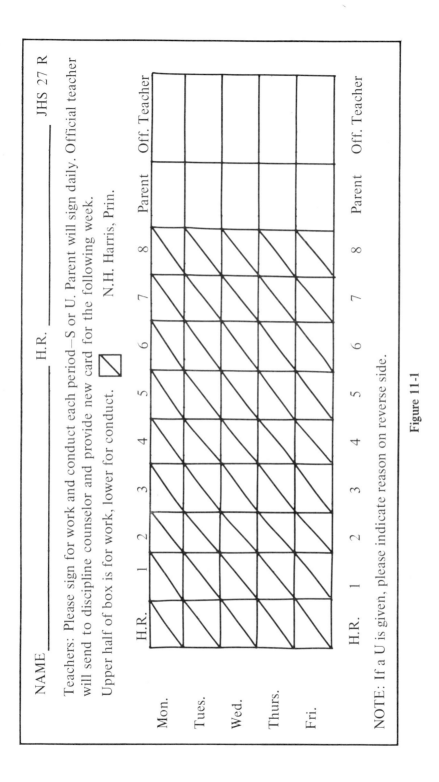

NAME _____ H.R. _____ JHS 27 R

Teachers: Please sign for work and conduct each period—S or U. Parent will sign daily. Official teacher will send to discipline counselor and provide new card for the following week.

Upper half of box is for work, lower for conduct. ⬚   N.H. Harris, Prin.

	H.R.	1	2	3	4	5	6	7	8	Parent	Off. Teacher
Mon.											
Tues.											
Wed.											
Thurs.											
Fri.											
	H.R.	1	2	3	4	5	6	7	8	Parent	Off. Teacher

NOTE: If a U is given, please indicate reason on reverse side.

Figure 11-1

day showing, every child was able to attend. By the second showing, some of the children had to be excluded. By the third, most
were back. (It had to be proved to the youngsters that attendance
at the "festival" was a reward, and anyone who didn't deserve to
attend did not. One teacher kept the uncooperative youngsters in
his room working while the other two supervised the group seeing
the film in the auditorium.)

Rewards may be as simple as a note home: "Johnny completed an excellent paper today. I wanted to let you know immediately because I know you'll be as delighted as I was."

One teacher gave out candy kisses. Of course, everyone in the
class earned one.

We have used a daily report card which has proved to be quite
effective in the sixth, seventh, and eighth grades. It enables each
teacher with whom the child comes into contact to grade him on a
daily basis. The parent is asked to sign this card each day to prove
that he or she has seen it. In this way, good work and conduct are
indicated and immediate gratification is achieved. (Many times
youngsters are given "conduct cards" after they have been
suspended or their parents called in for conferences because of bad
behavior. However, children will sometimes request to be "put on
a conduct card.")

How to Help the Disruptive Child
Set Goals for Himself

In the conference you have with your disruptive child to
develop your plan, begin by setting up goals. We have had excellent results with the experimental approach. "I have an experiment I must conduct," you tell the child. "I need one child (or
several, depending on the number of youngsters with whom you
wish to work) to work with me on this. Would you like to try?"
Most will agree readily. (Remember that this conference never
takes place while you're angry or upset.) Even the skeptical child
will usually want to participate. I believe that setting goals is very
important and that if a young person sets goals himself he can
usually reach them. "What seems to be the problem?" you ask the
child. You certainly know what it is. The question is—does he?

"I have to stay in my seat," Billy answers.

"Right!" you respond. "What else?"

"I have to stop yelling."

"Right again! What about your work?"

"I don't finish it."

"Let's work on that!"

Prepare a ditto master—a half page is usually enough. On it place the following:

Goal Sheet

_____ Child's Name (Write it in for each child for whom you are preparing a goal sheet)

Date _____   Subject _____

Goal:

Then have the child fill in the work he feels that he can accomplish. For example, the class has been assigned to write a composition of three paragraphs. This youngster feels that he can write only two. He therefore indicates on the sheet: Composition, two paragraphs. If the class has been assigned 15 examples for homework and he sets his goal at 12, that would be indicated. Do not accept less that 70% of the work assigned to the class unless you have a special reason for doing so.

Note here that the emphasis is on achievement. It is almost as if you are ignoring the disruptive behavior because what you're stressing is the work to be done—accentuating the positive.

Each time a child achieves his goal, write an "A" or a "100%" on his paper, staple his goal statement to it, and place it in his portfolio. Keeping a record in this way is another means of accentuating the positive.

Will you be ignoring the getting up and calling out? Not at all. On another of the goal sheets indicate: Do not call out. Stay in seat. At the end of the day give a letter grade for each of these.

Encourage your disruptive child to work for "all A's." A week of A's certainly deserves formal recognition—a letter home, a phone call, and so on.

How to Use Contracts to Set Goals

We have seen disruptive children react well to "contracts." We use contracts as a tool to enforce rules or regulations. They are used with serious offenders. When a child has been smoking, we have a contract stating: "I hereby promise that I will not smoke in the school building again. If I do, I will be placed in a class one grade lower than the one I am in until my parents come to school for a conference."

We have the contract typed and have each child sign three copies—one for himself, one for the dean, and one for the teacher.

Incidentally, we've shown parents the contract, after it was broken, on a number of occasions. Their reaction has been, "But you've been warned. You don't deserve another chance." Of course children deserve another chance, and another! That's what we are here for—to teach them—and sometimes it takes considerably more than one lesson to get an idea across.

When you want to use a contract, make everything in it feasible. If you have a youngster who is a compulsive talker (and there are such children, who are almost unaware of the fact that they are speaking) you cannot expect him or her to stop talking. However, in your contract limit the talking to certain times of the day.

I once took a class on a trip to a museum. One of the boys threw something at the driver. I told him that if he did that again he could never go on another school trip because he endangered the lives of all of us. He waited a while and then actually did it again. I had made a contract with him. I met him about 15 years later. He was now an over-the-road truck driver, and he asked: "Don't you remember me? You told me I'd never go on another trip, and I never did." Of course I remembered, and I said so.

"I just want you to know that you were right. I was a dumb kid. We could all have gotten killed. I'm glad I met you, so I could tell you."

"Tell me what?" I asked.

"That about three years ago I finally forgave you. Up until I started driving I never did."

Children respect firmness and authority if it is coupled with understanding. Without firmness and authority, a teacher is lost.

How to Obtain Parental Cooperation

Parents need to know what's going on in school. If a child is disruptive, he certainly isn't going to tell them. In fact, we've often seen children distort the truth, and while it would be nice to believe that they do so unwittingly, I'm afraid that this is not always so.

How can you let parents know? One simple way is to let parents see the results of work—homework, classwork, tests. Have the youngsters take the papers home to be signed. One teacher friend argued with me about this.

"The parents will be annoyed," she said.

"No they won't!" was my answer. Parents want to know.

In one particular class, which has far more than its share of disruptive children, the teacher uses a weekly report card. It has a space for a grade for work and one for conduct. It's sent home on Monday, the parents sign it, and it's due back on Tuesday.

"I've found that this has helped me get these youngsters to use self-control. Before I instituted this system, I always had laryngitis from screaming. Now it's no longer necessary."

Almost every school system has some form of parent-teacher conference week. Ours is called "Open School Week." However, it is almost always the parents of the hard workers who come in. To get to see the parents of the disruptive children, try writing a note to all parents, such as the following:

Dear

Please excuse the fact that this note is duplicated, but I would like very much to see the parents of every child in my class. Won't you please come in to school, to room ____ between _____ and _____ on _____.

I'm looking forward to talking to you. If you can't make it then, I would be happy to set up another appointment.

I know that by working together we can do a great deal to help your child.

Sincerely yours,

Mail these letters. If your school does not have funds for postage, mail only those which go to the parents of disruptive children. School notices advising parents rarely get home. If you were a disruptive child, would you take a notice home?

We have already discussed telephone calls, which are another highly effective technique for reaching parents. For a major problem, call in the evening, when both parents are probably at home. If you are not anxious to pull out your "big guns," an afternoon telephone call may be preferable.

Whichever form of communication you prefer, it is extremely important that you establish one. It is unbelievable how often a parent will say, "I never realized Betty was not doing her work," in spite of the fact that the child has brought home a report card which the parent signed!

How to Make Use of Guidance Services

If a child is disruptive, don't suffer in silence. About the same time you're having your first interview with him, notify the counselor. Keep an anecdotal record and be prepared to document your remarks.

In many schools disruptive children are not seen by the counselors because no teacher sends in referrals. This may sound incredible, but time after time we've asked if a referral to the counselor has been made. And the answer has been: "Not yet. I really should, I guess, but I haven't gotten round to it." Furthermore, don't get discouraged. Keep referring and writing notes! Even busy counselors will eventually take the hint.

When psychological examinations are needed, the paper work can be overwhelming, but it is worthwhile. Psychologically sick children do not belong in classrooms with well-adjusted children, and if it takes a ream of paper to get them placed properly, so be it.

We've found that those teachers who consult with the guidance counselor, or any other of the supportive personnel, get far better results than those who merely write notes. Conferences to discuss problems can be rewarding because of the ideas exchanged as well as the concrete action taken. Rapport between teachers and counselors is as important as rapport between teacher and youngster or counselor and youngster.

Often counselors will be the persons who manage to get the parents of the disruptive child to come in to school, and a three-way conference (parent-teacher-counselor) sometimes yields better results than a two-way one does.

The guidance counselor is usually the person who will do testing to determine whether a child needs special class placement. Often children who are retarded are very frustrated and become disruptive if they are in regular classes. Referrals must be made, and this is usually one of the tasks performed by the counselor.

How to Make Use of the Knowledge Previous Teachers Have to Offer

One of the best sources of information you have is a child's previous teacher.

"I'm having an awful time with Betty Lou Smith," the fifth grade teacher said.

"Oh, I can imagine," answered her fourth grade teacher. "Betty Lou was fine until her mother died. That was last year. She went all to pieces, and then she became very difficult in class."

Many things happen to "your" children when they are outside the school. Often you are unaware of them, but sometimes a previous teacher knows certain things which can be of help to you. Don't hesitate to ask.

"Billy Jones is causing a lot of grief," I heard one teacher say. "I really don't know how to reach him."

"Easy," said another. "I found that he wants to please his father. Tell him that if he cooperates, you'll write a note to his Dad."

Works like a charm! Each of us can be reached, and perhaps last year's teacher can give you the clue.

Check a youngster's record, too, for indications of where the problem lies. Often there will be only a comment such as "guidance conference with Mrs. Smith." Talk to the lady. It's almost guaranteed that you'll learn something.

We once had a real hell-raiser in class. We needed something to calm him and discovered from a previous teacher that there was one thing he loved to do more than anything else—he loved to operate a filmstrip projector. We made a "deal," and the disruption almost ceased. It's certainly worth a try. Talk to your colleagues when you need help with a particular child. However, form your own opinions—and realize that on occasion teachers' and youngsters' personalities may clash.

How to Determine the Cause of the Problem

Finding the causes of problems can be very difficult. This is especially true with children who are reluctant to discuss their feelings. However, there are several devices that you can use.

The autobiography is a good project for this purpose, but it may be too long and too time-consuming. But two compositions, "My Happiest Day" and "My Saddest Day," can reveal a great deal. So can the topic, "The Person I Admire Most." We do reveal much of ourselves in our writing, and this can give the perceptive teacher insight.

Puppet shows sometimes have the same effect. Youngsters who cannot express themselves directly are sometimes able to do so through puppets.

Sociodrama and open-ended plays are possible means of helping the child discuss his or her problems.

Parents, of course, can often tell you a great deal in this area—provided that they are not the cause of the problem. Even then, if you are perceptive, you can learn much about a family. Is the father domineering, and has the child adopted his behavior pattern? Or does the mother push the child so that he'll cheat to get high marks? Use your clinical eye during parent conferences, and many times you'll learn more than you expected to.

Standardized tests indicate ability and achievement. A review of a child's record can be helpful in determining whether his class placement is correct and if he is achieving in the manner he had previously.

The time you spend ferreting out the cause of a problem can pay big dividends in terms of changing a youngster's disruptive behavior.

How to Help the Disruptive Child to Change His Pattern of Behavior

People develop patterns of behavior which they tend to repeat—over and over again—if their psychological and/or physical needs are being met. A child who purposely doesn't eat lunch doesn't need as much food as one who can't wait for the meal. In the same way, a child who needs attention would rather get negative attention than none at all. To change the behavior pattern of your disruptive child, try to determine what his needs are and how he is fulfilling them.

The child who is loudest and most disruptive is often one who needs almost constant attention. If he is ignored by you and by the rest of the class and does not get the attention he craves, he will usually change his behavior pattern. Try moving him to the back of the room and, if possible, totally ignoring him. After a week of this, explain to him what you have been doing and why. Invite him back into the fold.

Of course, if you find a child's pattern of behavior must be changed, you will have gotten in touch with his parents. Parents are often willing to withdraw privileges if it is deemed necessary by the teacher. It's certainly worth a try.

We've found that changing seats often helps a great deal, particularly if you can move the disruptive child away from all of his friends. He must know that you will not accept disruptive behavior and will take action if it continues.

Still another technique you may try is holding "town hall" type discussions with the entire class in regard to behavior. Without mentioning names (although the youngsters usually do), discuss the need for cooperation on the part of every child in the class. There have been cases of youngsters who changed because they found that they were without allies. One very traumatic, but effective, incident occurred when a teacher received a note from the class signed by every child except one which asked for the transfer of that student. When the child discovered the contents of the note being circulated for signatures, he was very upset, and his behavior pattern did change.

When you do see changes, be lavish with your praise. Even a slight alteration is worth a comment.

Another technique which worked well was unusual. A teacher told me: "I had tried everything with this girl, Mary. Nothing worked. Then I had an idea. I called Mary's parents and said, 'She's been working beautifully. You can be proud of her.' Actually, she hadn't been doing any work at all, but after that call she began to work really hard. It was unbelievable!"

You can't tell if a technique will be effective until you try it.

The key, of course, is to set a course of action and follow it. The following list should be of help.

1. At the beginning of the year (or whenever you begin to teach a class), state the rules and regulations. You can work them out with the class, which is preferable, or simply state to the class the behavior you will accept. This must, however, be your word—and your bond.

2. At the first sign of disruption, refuse to accept the behavior. Try to correct it immediately by speaking to the child.

3. If further disruption occurs, hold a private discussion with the youngster to try to find out why he is being disruptive and to help him.

4. If the child continues with the same disruptive behavior, a note to the parents or a telephone call bringing it to their attention should be your next step.

5. Jot down notes regarding this behavior pattern so that you can discuss with the parents exactly (and non-judgmentally) the manner in which this youngster has been behaving.

6. Use your notes to discuss the youngster with the guidance counselor and/or your supervisor.

7. Try to give the disruptive child responsibility. However, do not reward negative behavior. Be sure that you do not give privileges to induce a child to curb his disruptive techniques, but rather as a result of his having curbed them.

8. Try giving the disruptive youngster a conduct card which is to be signed daily by both you and his parent. (Be sure that the parent is aware of the card and signs it. It is a simple matter for a youngster to sign the card himself.)

9. If you are able to establish a success pattern for the disruptive child by giving him work which he can complete and which gives him a feeling of accomplishment, you may be able to change his disruptive behavior pattern.

10. Check with the child's previous teachers for information which may be of help to you. A simple, "Tell me about Charles Smith. What's he interested in?" or "How can I reach him?" may elicit just the information you need.

11. Check into the child's previous records for information regarding family situation, mobility, and so on. A foster child who has been moved from home to home cannot be expected to show stability in his behavior pattern.

12. Use praise and rewards as often as you can. Every human being needs to feel self-worth, and the teacher is in a position to foster this. No action—be it a smile, a pat on the back, a friendly remark—is too slight to go unnoticed and unenjoyed.

Remember that your disruptive child is, after all, still a child who needs your love and understanding. When he's sure he has it, you may see a dramatic change in him, and the changes wrought this way—by a desire to please you—are always for the better!

Chapter 12

How to Deal with Children
Who Are Hyperactive, Psychologically Ill,
or Whose Self-Images Are Poor

How to Deal with the Hyperactive Child

Have you a youngster in your class who is so overactive that he disrupts the entire class? He's the one whose absence makes it possible to have a "beautiful class today." Many classes have such youngsters, and it's to this problem that the first portion of this chapter is addressed. The name usually associated with such children is "hyperactive." Hyperactive youngsters are not usually malicious, although their behavior often seems so. What begins as simple hyperactivity can annoy other children, and when they retaliate, there goes the ball game. Fights ensue, and the hyperactive child is often left wondering why.

It is virtually inevitable that the hyperactive child will become involved in incidents which will cause other youngsters to be annoyed or even furious with him or her. Simply running around the room, the hyperactive child may bump into a classmate and a verbal exchange may follow. What starts out as an outlet for energy results in ugliness which can be attributed to the actions of the hyperactive child. We once heard one child ask another, "Hey, what's the matter with you?" The second one, the hyperactive child, was immediately incensed at even that almost innocuous question. Bumping into another person, hitting him or her accidentally, breaking another's property—all of these are typical actions of the hyperactive, which he or she did not intend to create problems, but which inevitably do. It is asking too much of other youngsters to expect them to understand each time such an incident occurs. They may for a period of time, but they are children, and most lose their patience easily.

What You Can Do if You Have
Hyperactive Children in Your Class

As soon as the behavior manifests itself, call the parent in for an interview. You first step is to explain, in detail, the child's actions, without being judgmental. You should not say, "Johnny runs around this room as if he were a caged animal." Instead, say, "Johnny does not do his work. He tends to get up and move around the room several times an hour."

When you have such a child in your class and you realize you will need the parent's assistance, it is wise for you to keep a log of the child's activities for several days. This should consist of a brief notation of the time and the particular action. For example:

December 1, 1976—Johnny Jones

8:50— Refused to take seat when asked by me to do so.

9:15—Threw paper in wastebasket, then walked around the room.

9:40— Got up and spoke to Richard, whose seat is across the room.

9:45— John's work was not completed when it was collected.

10:05— Made loud noises. Stopped when I requested him to do so.

This type of report should be as objective as you can make it. Do not allow your emotions to enter into it.

As in all parent interviews, your approach should be: "What can we, working together, do to help your son?" We've found that this approach works in almost every case.

Explain hyperactivity to the parent and then question him or her for information regarding the child's behavior at home. A hyperactive child will rarely sit and watch television for hours. He or she is much more inclined to be on the move and to watch television only when other activities are not available. Even then, he or she usually finds something to do while watching—doodling, drawing, whittling, knitting, and so on.

Stress the fact that the hyperactivity is preventing the child from learning. A parent is far more interested in this than in the fact that the child is disturbing the rest of the children. Let's be realistic. We are, each of us, fundamentally interested in ourselves and in our children as extensions of ourselves. Therefore, stress your concern in terms of that child, not in terms of the rest of the class.

Be careful not to frighten the parent. If you do, he or she can turn on you. "That teacher said my child is sick," a parent reported. "That's not her job. Is she a doctor to tell me there's something wrong with my kid?" And, indeed, the parent was right. No teacher is legally qualified to diagnose, although many are able to do so with much accuracy. Be gentle with parents. If a child needs help and you use the right approach to explain the problem, his or her parent will do all he or she can do to get it. The danger lies in taking the wrong approach. A friendly concern cannot be misinterpreted.

Ask the parent to have the child examined by a physician. There are times when specific drugs may be prescribed by the doctor. There may be evidence of brain damage, for example, requiring special class placement. Still another possibility is diet.

How Food Additives May Affect Behavior

Recently, Dr. Ben Feingold, in his book *Why Your Child Is Hyperactive,* published by Random House, New York, related the cause of some hyperactivity in children to the fact that the child is affected by food additives. I admit that I personally was skeptical when news of this theory appeared in the newspapers. However, one teacher, whose word is certainly reliable, reported to me: "It's unbelievable. I have a boy in my class who was driving me out of my mind. I thought I'd never survive. Then I read about the food additive theory and bought a copy of the book. After I read it, I had a conference with the child's mother. She is very anxious to do anything she can to help. I loaned her my copy of the book. She agreed to put the child on the special diet, and it worked like magic. I forgot that the youngster had been a problem in the class. He did his work and behaved just like the other boys and girls. Then, almost as a test of the theory, came the Christmas holidays, and he went off the diet. The change in him was incredible. The old behavior patterns returned—exactly as if they had never disappeared. The running, the jumping, the calling out—all were back. I asked the boy if he had gone off his diet, and he very sheepishly admitted that he had. After the holiday season, he was put back on it. It isn't an easy diet for a youngster. All candy is eliminated, for instance. But he returned to it—and to normalcy. It's a diet which requires the strict cooperation of the parent and the child, but I found that it worked beautifully."

Refer the child for guidance services. Do not neglect to do this. So many times teachers say. "What can I do?" and throw their hands up in despair. The guidance department should be of help to you, even if the actual counseling does not seem to help the child very quickly. Often a hyperactive child needs an inordinate amount of attention, and guidance counselors can take part of this burden from you.

How to Help the Hyperactive Child Use up His Energy

Years ago a child of this type might have been called "nervous" as he or she sat and bit fingernails, fidgeted, and jumped around. Today, with a different climate in the classroom, the manifestations are vastly different, too. However, finding activity for this child can help him.

What can you do to have your hyperactive child use his time constructively and not disrupt the entire class?

Generally, hyperactive children have a very short attention span. This seems to be part of the pattern of behavior, and to really help such a child your first step is to study that behavior pattern. Does the youngster begin his or her work when instructed to do so? After a few minutes, does he or she lose interest? Or isn't the work begun at all? After you've answered those questions you have a clue. Give him work to do in small doses. Give him five examples instead of ten, for instance.

The next point to look for is this: Does the child listen to classwork at all, and if so, for how long? If he will "tune in" to your work, even for five minutes, you have something to work with. If not, that is a point of departure. Find something in which he is interested and begin work on that topic.

Hyperactive children are not hostile, particularly at the beginning of the school term, and often not during it, either. However, as we mentioned, this may change. But you should begin a campaign with this child by speaking to him or her privately, when you are not emotionally upset.

How to Deal with Children
Who Are Psychologically Ill

Unless you are a brand-new teacher, you have probably dealt with youngsters who you felt were "sick." You were probably right. There is much mental illness among the general public, and we certainly encounter the condition in our classrooms. Coping with the psychologically ill child can be one of the most exhausting, enervating of all tasks. What can we do to help you? There are a number of steps to be taken which you will find will make a difference.

How to Use a Team Approach

When you encounter a youngster with whom you are having great difficulty—be he overaggressive or withdrawn, hyperactive or totally lethargic—it is wise to think immediately of using a team approach. There are many people you'll involve—including your supervisor, the guidance counselor, the school psychologist, the parents, and other teachers. You are not alone in dealing with problem children, and knowing that assistance is available can be of great psychological help to you.

How does this illness reveal itself? In some cases the behavior of the child is highly bizarre. The child tries to hurt himself or other children. One youngster actually used matches to burn initials into her skin. Another boy spit into the faces of most adults with whom he came into contact. In other cases, the child may be very withdrawn and remote. Such children are often overlooked because they are not demanding of the teacher's time and attention. However, they do erupt, often with dire consequences.

Mentally ill youngsters need your love and affection more than other children. They may be your best friends and then suddenly turn on you, which can prove highly disturbing to you. But the problem is that they are not normal and do not function as normal persons.

One very interesting thing about serious mental illness is that often the illness is only manifested in one area of behavior. You've probably heard of men or women who think that they are Napoleon. They function perfectly normally in all areas except those related to being Napoleon. Since it is difficult to know what is going on in your students' minds, you cannot tell when their behavior will change—going off in any direction.

When you have reason to believe that a child is ill, check with his or her previous teachers. They, too, can be of help, both in giving you the history of the particular child and also by sharing with you those methods which they found were successful in working with that child.

If a child behaves in your class with any type of bizarre or unusual behavior, if he or she causes physical harm to himself or herself or others, if he or she is not "with it," consider the possibility of this youngster being psychologically ill and plan to work with him or her accordingly. Follow your impulses. They are based on your observations of many clues—some so slight that you are not even aware of them. Others will be so blatant that you can't ignore them even if you try. But if you have a psychologically ill youngster in your class, don't expect that child to behave normally. The day will come when he or she won't. Be ready for it. In that case, removing that child from the class may be the only alternative. That removal may be temporary or permanent, depending on the child's condition and the facilities available.

Notify your supervisor, either in writing or verbally, as soon as you are sure that the child is disturbed. At this point you're not asking for action, you are merely bringing the case to the attention of the administration. Ask for suggestions, because it is entirely possible that the supervisor can be of help to you. He or she may have dealt with this youngster previously or may have experience in dealing with children with this particular problem.

How to Be Ever Watchful—Because You Must Be

Why must you be ever watchful?

1. To prevent untoward incidents from occurring. In one school a youngster climbed onto the window sill of a fifth floor room and was threatening to jump out of the window. Fortunately, the teacher grabbed him before he got out of the window and was able to hold him until help came.

2. To be able to obtain help for the youngster, you will need detailed notes describing exactly what he or she did. These notes, usually referred to as "Anecdotals," will be described subsequently. They should include the date the incident took place and a brief description of it. You'll need these notes when you speak to the parents, the guidance department, and your supervisor.

Your watchfulness should include:

1. Observations of the child's behavior
   A. In class—under normal working conditions.
   B. In class—when the child is under pressure. This would include while tests were being given.
   C. In the lunchroom—when children are under a minimum of supervision (and when many incidents occur because of this).
   D. In the gymnasium—while games are in progress. (This is another time when psychological illness will show.)

2. Another area in which psychological problems are sometimes revealed is written work. Topics such as "My Happiest Day" or "My Saddest Day" may result in stories which indicate deep troubles. We recently had a case of a boy writing about his mother's death, of his suspecting foul play, and his preparations to avenge the "murder." The entire story was fantasy—a product of the child's imagination—but, accompanied by other symptoms, proved to be an indication of psychological illness. (The mother had left the home but was not dead. The child had seen her the week before he wrote the composition.)

Another indication of possible illness is doodling if a child draws lethal weapons—guns, knives, and so on. This indication of hostility should never be overlooked. Indicate it to the guidance counselor or to your supervisor. This child bears watching!

How to Cope (Even Temporarily) with Children Who Are Psychologically Ill

Try to learn, from your own observation, from the parent, from the counselor, and from the administration, what sets the child off. We've heard the expression many times, "Robert (or Joe, Bill, or Mary) has a very short fuse." But something lights the fuse. Try to find out what it is. If it's the full moon, there isn't too much you can do.

We've seen one particular set of circumstances repeated with various children many times. When a child lives with foster parents and his natural mother comes to visit him, after she leaves the youngster often goes into a very highly agitated state. The repeated rejection is so deadly that the youngsters can't cope with it. This is just one possible family problem. There are countless others.

When a child is psychologically ill, the "trigger" is extremely difficult to find, but it will be very helpful for you to discover it.

Find a holding action. As suggested above, you've already alerted the administration and the counselor. Therefore, if you feel the child is going to "flip out," you must find a "holding action" for him. A possible holding action would be to send the child to either the counselor or the administrator for a limited length of time.

On a number of occasions, youngsters have said to me, "I'm going to have a fight today." Of course, if they tell you they will—they surely will! Happens every time. One possible method for handling this is to assign the child to a different class for the day—*if he agrees.* If he doesn't agree, don't even try. Another method, if permissible in your school system, is to telephone the parents and, with their permission, send the child home. This "cooling off period" can prevent serious difficulties. Sometimes a talk with the child will help—if you can determine the problem. Often there is nothing you can do about it, but your show of understanding can help.

If this child is "set off" by other specific youngsters, try to separate him from these children. Children often love to tease, and this can cause the ill child a great deal of mental torture. The fact is that these ill children are often the "goats" of the class for the simple reason that the others have learned exactly how to get them to react. Instead of reacting with tears, which they cometimes do, they more often become enraged. Therefore, try to place your special problem children right near your desk and away from youngsters who will cause them to create serious incidents.

When a child is agitated, it is essential that he be removed from the classroom situation as quickly as possible. However, if this cannot be done, you might try a technique used by guidance counselor Mrs. Helen Harris. She asked the disturbed child to make confetti. This involved tearing pages of old telephone books into confetti-sized paper. If you do not have these books, any paper, even newspaper, will do. Seat the child by himself and supply the paper and a container in which to put the confetti. There is no need for you to explain what it will be used for. Just say, "Would you please make some confetti for me?" Mrs. Harris discovered that this procedure had a calming effect on agitated children and enabled her to get them cooled down to a point where it was possible to talk with them.

Permanent removal of the psychologically ill child depends on the action taken by the school administration.

How to Work with Children
Whose Self-Images Are Poor

Ask any adult you know if he or she can remember one particular teacher. It is a very rare person who does not. Some teachers have a very marked effect on their students. One of the ways you can have that effect is by working with children whose self-image is poor, helping them to develop a better image of themselves. The child with a poor self-image is almost doomed to drag through life, accepting its crumbs; however, your efforts can sometimes help to change this.

Working with a child whose self-image is poor can be extremely rewarding to the compassionate teacher. There are a number of steps which can be taken:

1. Find out where the child's strengths are and build on those. This may take time. However, it may be learned in a "rap session" with the child. One boy, Larry, whose attendance record in school left much to be desired, revealed to his teacher that he liked working with tin cans. Larry made lanterns, toys, and such objects as coasters and ash trays, and was asked to participate in the school's annual fair. After he made many samples, he was asked if he'd like a booth of his own. He became the school expert in metal work, and positive changes in his personality became evident. His self-image improved dramatically, as did his attendance.

2. Make the child a monitor whenever you can, without being too obvious about it. Find tasks that he or she can do efficiently and assign them to the youngster.

3. Voice your approval of his or her achievements whenever you can. A smile, a pat on the shoulder, a remark, "Gee that's fine!" can all help this youngster to feel better about himself or herself.

When you can, give him or her a note of commendation, a letter, or any sort of symbol to take home. This concrete evidence can help the youngster to have a better feeling about himself or herself, and by showing your approval to his or her family, you can sometimes improve a negative opinion of the child in his or her own home.

4. Help the child to develop better communication skills. Almost every child suffering from a poor self-image needs help in this area. Rarely do you find a person with the ability to speak well who feels negatively about himself. Probably the best way to develop this skill is to get the child to talk—about himself or herself or about anything else. Talking privately with the youngster is well worth the time.

5. One of the best techniques for teaching self-expression is the use of buzz groups, where each person contributes to the discussion of a topic. Divide your class into five or six buzz groups. Be sure to put the dominant personalities in one group, the more quiet in another. In this way, you can structure the situation so that the child with the poor self-image is put into the position where he *must* contribute. Give each group topics to discuss and then have the class reconvened. At that time have one member of the group report on the discussion. Don't neglect this feedback aspect. It, too, is important.

How to Build That Very Important
Success Pattern

When a child feels negatively about himself, the building of a success pattern can be one of the best projects on which you and that child can embark.

We had one child who did not attend school for a period of years. This posed many difficulties, among which the feeling of a lack of self-worth was probably the greatest. This child returned to school, at first on a part-time and then on a full-time basis. He had problems academically and was extremely reluctant to participate in class work. However, we were looking for material for the school literary publication, and it was then that we discovered the young man's ability to write poetry. His poems were simple but deeply moving, and he was able to convey much of his emotion in his work. The poems were the first step in breaking through his feelings of self-defeat. As we mentioned before, begin work with any youngster by determining his or her strength and developing it.

We have often seen youngsters with poor self-images being virtually ignored by the teacher, particularly when they are quiet and undemanding. It is these very children who need attention—positive, reinforcing attention.

Art, music, health education, all subjects offer opportunities for this reinforcement.

You can have your youngsters write compositions which can be graded in two ways. Grade for ideas and for written English. Again, we must repeat—any time, any attention, any positive reinforcement you give to the youngsters with poor self-images can help to change these negative feelings. If we have over-emphasized your role as the teacher in attempting to do this, it is because we are so certain that the actions you take can and do make a difference, and this difference, in turn, can lead to a much happier life for these children.

How to Give the Youngster
with a Poor Self-Image
Hope for the Future

The child with the poor self-image is the last youngster in the world who expects to go to college—and yet you can do much to change his or her feelings about himself or herself by showing that going to college is not only a dream but entirely possible. Here's how (incidentally, we have actually done this scores of times):

In "rapping" with the child, ask what his or her plans for the future are. Most of the time you will be greeted by a look of total blankness. In fact, these youngsters have often looked at me as if I've gone absolutely stark raving mad. No matter—you continue, "You know, if you decide that you want to attend college, you can. But you have to make up your mind—you have to decide that *you really want to go.* Once you've decided that, there is a lot of help available to you."

If you can convey this concept, that every young person who wants to go to college is able to do so because of certain colleges and because of the money the Federal government has made available, you can change attitudes—and lives.

It is very worthwhile to do this with young children because you can give them hope—if you speak to them on their level of comprehension.

For your own information, to be conveyed to children when you feel that they can use it, we are going to include a list of possibilities for a child with a minimum of funds to attend college.

How You Can Go to College!

1.   The community colleges (two-year colleges) located in every state of the union offer the first two years of a college education at very low tuition rates. (For the child who needs help with this, we'll discuss finances a bit later.)

The community colleges offer two types of program:

(a) A two-year liberal arts program, after which the student can transfer to a four-year college to earn a B.A. degree.

(b) A two-year career-oriented program which gives the student an A.A. (Associate of Arts) degree.

There is a huge variety of career training available in the two-year colleges.

2.   The four-year city or state college or university offers Bachelor degrees (Arts or Science). Training is available for some of the professions—teaching, engineering, accounting, to name three. Tuition is far less than at private colleges.

3.   Each branch of the Armed Forces has a program to suit the needs of most young people, which enables them to earn money and attend college while in the service.

4.   Many private colleges offer scholarships, but they must be applied for and far too often students do not bother doing so.

We said that we'd discuss sources of funds for a college education. There are a number of places it's available.

1.   We've already mentioned scholarships. They are applied for through the college's financial officer. Often, the scholarship is accompanied by a part-time job offer so that the young person is able to pay all or most of his way. A scholarship is a gift, which does not have to be repaid. The same is true of a grant.

Scholarships are given for scholastic ability and for many other reasons—athletics, music, and a variety of others. Scholarships are well worth checking out.

If the child's parents belong to a union or a fraternal organization, there is a chance that one of these organizations may offer scholarship assistance.

S. Norman Feingold's book on scholarships is a storehouse of information on this subject. Another excellent reference is Arco Publishing Company's "How to Obtain Money for College," by Wm. E. Lever. Published in 1976, it contains a tremendous amount of information (and only costs $5.00).

The American Legion publishes a booklet of scholarship information called "Need a Lift?" It is available for 50¢ from American Legion, Department S.P.O., Box 1055, Indianapolis, Ind. 46206. It's a real bargain!

2. Federal grants are given by the government to persons in need of financial help. How much a person receives depends on the family income. Even if a young man or woman attends a community college, he or she can still apply for and receive a grant to pay for food, clothing, lodging, and so on.

Grants are available no matter what college a person attends.

3. Student loans. If a person can't get enough money from a scholarship or a grant, he or she can always apply for a student loan. These loans do not have to be paid back until the student graduates.

4. The Veteran's Administration has special benefits for veterans; servicemen and women and their dependents; and for wives, widows, widowers, and children of disabled, missing, or deceased veterans.

If you have occasion to give guidance to a young person, the information above is basic to the situation. By giving it to him, you can change the course of his entire life.

Index